D1464783

HRM in Tourism and Hospitality

Also available from Cassell:

Boella and Pannett: *Principles of Hospitality Law*, 2nd edn

Forsyth: *Maximizing Hospitality Sales*

Godfrey and Clarke: *The Tourism Development Handbook*

Johns and Lee-Ross: *Research Methods in Service Industry Management*

Leask and Yeoman (eds): *Heritage Visitor Attractions*

O'Connor: *Using Computers in Hospitality*, 2nd edn

Ryan (ed.): *The Tourist Experience*

Thomas (ed.): *The Management of Small Tourism and Hospitality Firms*

HRM in Tourism and Hospitality

International Perspectives on Small to Medium-sized Enterprises

Edited by Darren Lee-Ross

CASSELL

Cassell
Wellington House
125 Strand
London WC2R 0BB

370 Lexington Avenue
New York
NY 10017–6550

www.cassell.co.uk

First published 1999

British Library Cataloguing-in-Publication Data
A catalogue record for this book is available from the British Library.

ISBN 0–304–70410–5 (hb)
    0–304–70411–3 (pb)

Typeset by ensystems, Saffron Walden, Essex
Printed by Redwood Books, Trowbridge, Wiltshire

Editor's Dedication and Acknowledgements

This book is dedicated to my wife Mandi, for her encouragement, faith and invaluable assistance. I would also like to thank my contributors for their diligence, patience and hard work, without which my editorial task would have been onerous.

Contents

PART THREE   OPERATIONS: BEST PRACTICE

The Contributors

EDITOR

Darren Lee-Ross currently teaches and researches in the areas of human resource management (HRM) and hospitality at James Cook University, Australia. His PhD is from Anglia Polytechnic University and his areas of specialism include attitudes and work motivation, and service quality. He has co-written a number of texts and has contributed many articles to books and journals in these areas.

CONTRIBUTORS

Tom Baum is Professor of International Hospitality Management and Head of Department of the Scottish Hotel School at the University of Strathclyde, Glasgow. His PhD is from the University of Strathclyde in the area of human resource management. Tom has researched and consulted in Europe, Asia, Australia, Africa, the Caribbean and North America, working on projects supported by a wide range of public and private sector funding agencies. His specialism is in the area of HRM, education and training for hospitality and tourism. He is the author or editor of six books and close to 100 scholarly papers. In addition to an academic career at the Universities of Ulster, Buckingham and Strathclyde, Tom gained eight years' applied hospitality sector experience, working in a co-ordination and advisory capacity in the area of training and HRM in the Irish hospitality industry.

Bonnie Farber Canziani is Lead Specialist in service operations auditing, customer service systems, train the trainer and survey design at the College of Business, San José State University. Her primary research interests are in the transport, hospitality and tourism sector. She is the co-author of several books and numerous articles in the areas of customer service and service operations analysis and training.

Julia Christensen Hughes is Associate Professor in the School of Hotel and Food Administration, University of Guelph, Canada. Her research interests include motivation, diversity, empowerment and organizational change.

Michael Davidson is a former general manager of a five-star hotel and the foundation Head of Griffith University's School of Tourism and Hotel Management.

He has published in the area of hospitality and tourism education and is completing a PhD in the area of organizational climate in the hotel industry. His teaching includes organizational behaviour, operations and conference management. Currently Michael is Director of Griffith University's Centre for Business Education and Development.

Taylor Ellis received his PhD from Texas A & M University and is Associate Professor at the University of Central Florida. He is currently teaching guest services and conducting research on the factors leading to customer satisfaction in the hospitality industry.

Szilvia Gyimóthy is a PhD student, based at the Research Center of Bornholm, Denmark, studying the way sequential service experiences at a holiday destination influence overall satisfaction. Szilvia's research aims to improve understanding of destination branding, marketing and extended quality management. Szilvia has presented her work at several conferences and published in a number of tourism-related books and journals.

Rick Holden is Principal Lecturer (Research) in the School of Human Resource Management, Leeds Metropolitan University, UK. In addition to the HR aspects of graduate employment, his research interests embrace organizational learning and lifelong learning. He is currently editor of the MCB journal *Education and Training*.

Stephanie Jameson is employed by the School of Tourism and Hospitality Management at Leeds Metropolitan University, UK. She is also a member of the Centre for the Study of Small Tourism and Hospitality Firms, Leeds Metropolitan University. Her research interests include human resource management, employment relations in small firms and graduate employment in small firms.

Nick Johns is currently Visiting Senior Research Fellow at the Research Centre of Bornholm, a Danish tourism institution. He holds an Associate Reader post at Queen Margaret College, Edinburgh as well as a professorship with the International Management College's University for Industry – Hospitality Worldwide initiative. Nick has extensive national and international teaching and research experience, specifically in service quality management and business development. Nick has written several books and contributed numerous articles to books and journals in the service quality field. His innovative ideas have prompted widespread discussion in the service management field.

Jay Kandampully is currently Senior Lecturer in Services Management and Hospitality at Lincoln University, Canterbury, New Zealand. His PhD was in 'Total quality management through continuous improvement in service industries' and he has nine years' international hotel management experience. His research publication on the concept of 'service loyalty' earned him the prestigious international Literati Award for the most outstanding paper of the year 1997, published in the journal *Managing Service Quality*. Jay also received the 1998 Lincoln University Fund for Excellence Award for his research in service industry management.

Amanda Lee-Ross is a former owner/operator of two small businesses. She has an honours degree in Politics (York University) and a postgraduate diploma in management from Sheffield Hallam University. Amanda has extensive management experience within both the health service and hospitality sector. Recently she tutored in HRM and communication studies at the Centre for Professional Development in Club Management, Southern Cross University, Australia, before returning to England where she is currently employed as Commissioning Manager for Research, Wessex Institute for Health Research and Development, Southampton University.

Abraham Pizam is Professor of Tourism Management in the department of Hospitality Management and Director of the Dick Pope Sr Institute for Tourism Studies at the University of Central Florida in Orlando, Florida, USA. Professor Pizam teaches and conducts research in the areas of tourism human resources management and tourism marketing.

Nils Timo is a former industrial advocate for the Australian Workers' Union in the area of tourism and hospitality. He has negotiated over 100 workplace agreements within the industry. His PhD was in 'Employment relations in the hotel industry'. Currently Nils lectures at Griffith University in the areas of employment relations and workplace change. His current research is examining management practice and labour markets in hotels.

Abbreviations

AIC	Australian Industry Commission
AIRC	Australian Industrial Relations Commission
DfEE	Department for Education and Employment (UK)
EHE	Enterprise in Higher Education
GNVQ	General National Vocational Qualification
HR	Human Resource
HRD	Human Resource Development
HRIS	Human Resource Information System
HRM	Human Resource Management
IiP	Investors In People
IT	Information Technology
NVQ	National Vocational Qualification
SME	Small to Medium-sized Enterprise
SVQ	Scottish Vocational Qualification
TEC	Training and Education Council
TEP/TEI	Tourism Education Policy/Tourism Education Implementation
TTS	Tourism Training Scotland
VAT	Value Added Tax
VQ	Vocational Qualification

Introduction

DARREN LEE-ROSS

Over recent years the international market-place for the tourism and hospitality industry has become increasingly dynamic and competitive. Environmental conditions of globalization, deregulated labour markets and changing demographic profiles make the management of service delivery increasingly problematic. In particular, these shifting environmental conditions have led to difficulties for many smaller firms; they can no longer rely on regional or even national markets for survival. The situation where many small sellers compete among themselves is rapidly being eroded by the dominance of multinational corporations and the higher incidence of mergers and take-overs. Thus, traditional characteristics of low concentration and ease of entry are becoming a thing of the past. The nature of demand has also changed. Increasingly, service providers are faced with better educated, well-travelled and altogether more sophisticated consumers. This translates into higher customer expectations, and organizations must ensure they provide a service which satisfies these new consumer dynamics. Organizational success will therefore depend heavily upon the management of service provision that acknowledges the essential role employees play in service delivery.

To maximize the chances of success, organizations must seek competitive advantage. Many international corporations have attempted to do this by redefining their product and targeting specific customer segments. As a result, there have been some significant changes in service products. For example, an increase of budget-type accommodation has emerged both in Europe and the UK. Other corporations have done similarly by redefining elements of their service product portfolio or by downsizing their workforce – thereby encouraging customers to take part in their own service provision. These companies have also invested in new recruitment, selection and training procedures for their employees.

Clearly the former and potentially more expensive options are less feasible for small organizations with limited resources. This may disadvantage them in a number of ways. In addition, small to medium-sized tourism and hospitality enterprises (SMEs) have other inherent characteristics which may impact negatively upon service quality and subsequent competitive success. For example, they offer jobs that have limited prospects of career progression and a feeling of transience because of cyclical demand fluctuations. Thus, many jobs are part time with poor rates of pay. In addition, management styles tend to be despotic and non-supportive of workers. These issues help to create an unstable workforce where employees are difficult to recruit and retain. A combination of these conditions and characteristics is likely to have a damaging effect on service quality.

Scope and definition

In the UK since 1971, there have been uniform increases in service industry employment compared with an equal and opposite decline in manufacturing jobs. Along with the increasing economic stature of the service sector, small to medium-sized firms are also recognized as having a significant role to play in terms of providing employment and wealth generation. In the UK, past and present governments have introduced initiatives designed to establish and encourage growth of small firms (for example, see Bolton, 1971; Goss, 1991; Stanworth and Gray, 1991). This impact has been particularly substantial in the tourism and hospitality industry because it is dominated by smaller firms.

After reviewing the data, Boer, Thomas and Webster (1997) conclude that small firms in the UK are numerous but there is no central structure to collate information and that interpretations of the SME sector depend on assumptions of different researchers. Thus, definitions of SMEs vary dramatically depending upon research focus. Work centred upon tourism and hospitality SMEs does little to standardize the position (for example, see Quinn, Larmour and McQuillan, 1992; Storey, 1994). Many definitions have been criticized at some time or other for reasons of 'inappropriateness' and complexity. For example, the Bolton Committee definition is criticized because its financial criterion fails to account for inflation, and the employee number benchmark used (200) conflicts with its prescribed management style (personalized). Storey (1994) concludes that although there are a number of definitions of SMEs, that of the European Union (EU) is most useful because the definitive criterion is number of employees. In brief, the EU recognizes three categories of 'small' organization:

- *micro enterprises* fewer than 10 employees
- *small enterprises* between 10 and 99 employees
- *medium-sized enterprises* at least 100 but fewer than 500.

The advantage of such an apparently simple approach is that it allows measurable international comparisons. However, for the purposes of hospitality SMEs it is inappropriate, particularly for hotels because there are usually fewer employees per organization compared with those of other industries. This weakness is recognized tacitly in a report by the Hospitality Training Foundation (1996), who consider tourism and hospitality SMEs small, small to medium and large according to the following:

- *small* between 1 and 10 employees (87 per cent);
- *small to medium-sized* between 11 and 24 employees (10 per cent);
- *large* at least 25 employees (3 per cent).

This is a more appropriate classification system and shows that SMEs in this sector currently employ 97 per cent of the UK tourism and hospitality workforce.

Ownership

Tourism and hospitality SMEs tend to be under-capitalized and thus have limited finance for marketing, facility improvement and expansion. Ownership usually takes the form of 'sole proprietor', 'partnership' or, in some cases, 'private limited company'. Some entrepreneurs choose to join marketing co-operatives or become part of a franchise. Co-operatives such as Golden Chain, Budget and Best Western provide marketing and referral services for smaller operators who pay a fee per room and operate their properties autonomously, provided agreed minimum standards are maintained.

Direct tourist income generated by the smaller enterprise is often viewed as a valuable input to local economies. Government authorities and local hotel owner associations may assist smaller organizations. This takes a number of forms including direct grants, subsidized loans and 'partnerships' between public and private sector for regional promotions, advertising and purchasing.

Research and human resource management

Despite a minor shift of interest toward SMEs, there is still a paucity of research, especially that dealing with human resource issues. On the one hand, owner/managers are suspicious of researchers' motives; on the other, researchers are less keen to work in unconventional organizations whose strategies, operations and policies challenge contemporary management thinking. According to Storey (1994) this situation has led to an unclear understanding of SMEs and particularly of employment and employee relations.

It is a mistake to assume that small firms are simply smaller versions of their larger counterparts. Small businesses are usually driven by one or two people and are likely to have cultures, strategies and objectives which are complex and different from those of larger firms. Boer *et al.* (1997) consider that human resources matters in SMEs are characterized by a number of elements including the following:

- employees tend to be young, poorly qualified, recruited from the 'secondary' labour market and with an unstable work history, because hotels offer unskilled occupations, low pay, temporary and part-time work and have high levels of labour turnover;
- low union representation, occupational communities having interests conflicting with those of the organization;
- managers who are autocratic, paternalistic, impulsive and unpredictable;
- dominance of workforce by family members (owners).

In addition, tourism and hospitality SMEs have other defining characteristics which set them apart from large organizations. Some small firms have a short life cycle whereas others may grow slowly and flourish. Highly seasonal demand patterns create enormous pressure on owners and their workers to generate turnover and profits to tide them over quiet periods. In the UK seasonal seaside sector, the 'off' season can be of six to eight months' duration. Owner/managers of tourism and hospitality SMEs may be unqualified and inexperienced in service provision. Often in such cases, day-to-day operations appear chaotic, unplanned and unco-ordinated.

Interestingly, many tourism and hospitality SMEs remain successful. Typically, this depends upon their ability to adapt to environmental shifts by being creative, innovative and redefining their objectives. This can also depend on their recognition that they are different from large corporations and have their own distinctive characteristics. Indeed, recent growth in this sector has been encouraged in many countries because of prevailing political 'enterprise' philosophy, fragmentation of large firms and technological change. In most cases organizations have undergone a process of redevelopment in order to conceptualize a clear vision for the future. They have adopted strategies whereby workers are viewed as an essential part of the product. It is recognized that employees have a key impact upon 'added value' and service quality instead of being simply providers or deliverers of the product. In sum, coherent labour strategies and a culture of flexibility have allowed some hospitality and tourism SMEs to succeed where others have failed.

Typically, owner/managers of tourism and hospitality SMEs operate in a diverse and dynamic business environment. As such, they need to be able to function effectively at a number of different levels (often simultaneously). This book reflects the inherent complexity of SMEs and provides information useful for a wide range of operational and strategic situations. In other words, this text should allow entrepreneurs to make better informed practical and long-term decisions about human resources in their organizations. The contents are divided into three parts with ten chapters of approximately 6500 words each. Part One contains four chapters which provide a broad view of the international tourism and hospitality SME environment. In Chapter 1, Tom Baum explores the HRM challenges faced by tourism and hospitality SMEs and considers the supportive governmental role required to maintain and enhance service delivery standards. Nils Timo and Mike Davidson narrow the focus in Chapter 2 by considering the labour market for Australian hotels; trends in HRM practice; implications for future labour use and its impact upon service quality. Jay Kandampully provides a rigorous analysis of service quality in Chapter 3. He discusses HRM-based service considerations essential for the creation and maintenance of competitive advantage in tourism and hospitality SMEs of New Zealand. Part One concludes with Rick Holden and Stephanie Jameson's identification of critical issues in the employment and utilization of graduates in hospitality SMEs. In Chapter 4 they raise a number of questions about the graduation and employment process in relation to the assumption that the future for graduates within hospitality will be dominated by small firms.

Chapters contained in Part Two concentrate upon important HRM-based organizational issues for tourism and hospitality SMEs. In Chapter 5, Julia Christensen Hughes positions the crucial role of employee motivation and its impact on service quality by providing a comprehensive review of contemporary motivation theories. She points out the importance of front-line employee motivation and its immediate impact on customer satisfaction and also the motivational impact of worker culture and heterogeneity. Bonnie Farber Canziani highlights the increasingly important role of information technology (IT) for many functions of HRM in tourism and hospitality SMEs. Chapter 6 continues with a systematic exploration of the use of IT, suggesting that adoption will result in an efficient and effective delivery of human resources services. In Chapter 7, Abraham Pizam and Taylor Ellis examine the well documented problem of absenteeism and labour turnover in hospitality SMEs. They familiarize us with the most current information related to turnover and absenteeism and point out that the increasingly high cost of employee replacement must drive managers to understand the causes and effects so they can reduce the occurrence of each.

Part Three provides examples of best practice from distinct tourism and hospitality perspectives. In Chapter 8, Amanda Lee-Ross overviews the UK public house sector. Managing change and team-building are highlighted as two frequent and challenging roles for pub managers. In particular, the co-ordination of existing staff by new managers is represented as an important but ignored facet of pub management. The relevance of existing change management and team-building theories is questioned and it is argued that small organizations have no bureaucratic 'comfort buffer' between change agents and employees. In addition, the often one-dimensional perspective of change agents is challenged. She argues, with practical recommendations, that if effective change is to take place, the feelings and aspirations of change agents must be considered alongside those of employees. Part Three continues by providing examples of best practice from tourism and hospitality perspectives featuring case studies from each sector. Chapter 9 features three examples of tourism SMEs in which Nick Johns and Szilvia Gyimóthy describe ownership, employment structures and HRM practices and policies. In Chapter 10, Darren Lee-Ross summarizes the development of UK seasonal seaside resorts. In addition, he evaluates a variety of contemporary environmental influences upon the employment of seasonal hotel workers and provides a number of practical workable recommendations at strategic and co-ordinative managerial levels.

REFERENCES

Boer, A., Thomas, R. and Webster, M. (1997), *Small Business Management*. London: Cassell.

Bolton, J. (1971), *Report of the Committee of Inquiry on Small Firms*. London: HMSO.

Goss, D. (1991), *Small Business and Society*. London: Routledge.

Hospitality Training Foundation (1996), *Catering and Hospitality Industry – Key Facts and Figures*. London: HTF.

Quinn, U., Larmour, R. and McQuillan, N. (1992), The small firm in the hospitality industry. *International Journal of Contemporary Hospitality Management*, **4** (1), 11–14.

Stanworth, J. and Gray, C. (1991), *Bolton 20 Years On: The Small Firm in the 1990s*. London: Paul Chapman.

Storey, D. (1994), *Understanding the Small Business Sector*. London: Routledge.

PART ONE
Environment

CHAPTER ONE

Human Resource Management in Tourism's Small Business Sector: Policy Dimensions

Tom Baum

INTRODUCTION

The tourism sector, world-wide, consists of an amalgam of public and private sector concerns operating across a diversity of supply-side sub-sectors (accommodation, transport, attractions, facilitation etc.) and catering for visitors with widely differing needs and expectations. The supply side, as well as exhibiting variation in terms of operational characteristics, includes businesses that vary in size and scope of operation from the mega-corporation, present on six continents (for example, Accor, American Express, the Star airline alliance), to micro-businesses, employing a handful of staff and meeting visitor needs at a local resort level.

A common denominator for all these businesses, large and small, is their reliance on quality personnel in order to deliver their products and services to an increasingly demanding consumer market-place. With the technological and communicational capacity to deliver common product standards on a global basis, tourism sector providers need to focus on the delivery of service quality in order to attain a competitive edge. In order to achieve this, investment in all stages of human resource management (HRM) is essential – recruitment, selection, training, ongoing development. For large corporations, this commitment is reflected in significant investment in human resource (HR) infrastructure, systems and expertise, including the establishment of dedicated universities, training facilities and electronic delivery mechanisms. These organizations also tie in closely with major colleges and universities world-wide, in order to recruit high-quality graduates into their corporate ranks. Trends towards an increasingly active role for the private sector in meeting its educational and training requirements from school level onwards can be found in the University for Industry concept in the UK as well as in dedicated 'universities' operated by major corporations such as Disney and Accor. By contrast, small businesses in tourism, as in other sectors of the economy, do not necessarily have the capacity, capability, resources or commitment to support the human resource development (HRD) function in a manner that would enable them to compete effectively with larger organizations. Furthermore, the frequent geographical dispersal of small tourism operations in remote and peripheral locations also inhibits their ability to link effectively into existing main-stream public or private HRD provision. In many respects, the relative challenges facing micro-tourism businesses in the HR area relative to large companies have direct parallels to those which confront the same organiza-tions in terms of their marketing and, to some extent, operations as well (Morrison, 1998a; Ogden, 1998).

This chapter explores the challenges which small tourism businesses face in the area of HRM and considers the policy and role, if any, which government can play in supporting small tourism businesses to maintain and enhance their service delivery standards through HRD. In addressing these issues, it is important to recognize that the debate will impinge upon concerns which are at the heart of the fiscal and monetary policies of many governments in the developed and developing world in that they relate to what role, if any, public sector funding should play in supporting business development, especially through education and training. There are no clear, definitive responses to this question and those that may be used by way of illustration are closely allied to political judgement and ideological positioning.

The case for state involvement in HRM for tourism

The case for state involvement with tourism, particularly in the area of HRD, includes arguments that are primarily structural and developmental in nature. Despite the growing importance of large organizations within some sectors of tourism (notably accommodation, attractions, retail and transportation), tourism remains dominated by small to medium-sized enterprises (SMEs) which are frequently independently owned and oper-ated. However, the nature of tourism distribution means that even where multinational presence is in evidence the actual business units may well be small and may operate within a variety of different business formats, notably franchise arrangements. Small businesses, in general, can face a distinct disadvantage in the area of HRD, although this is not necessarily always the case. The lack of critical mass in employment terms and the tendency not to carry specialist management in HR or training mean that such functions, if they are to be executed, must be the responsibility of managers and supervisors who have a range of other functions within the organization. Specialism, in itself, is no guarantee that a function will be carried out to good effect but it does, at least, ensure that resources are in place to meet some of an organization's requirements in this area. The other major justification for public sector involvement in supporting the HRD needs of tourism businesses is particularly relevant in the context of developing tourism economies (Esichaikul and Baum, 1998) because the tourism sector does not have the maturity, cohesiveness, expertise or level of international investment to meet its HRD needs unaided. In particular, the absence of a strong private sector is a reason used to justify the support role of government in the HR area in developing countries.

In a general sense, there are political, environmental and economic reasons why the public sector can be involved in tourism (Wanhill, 1997, 1998). As Inskeep (1991) points out, the nature of this involvement needs to be adapted to the particular needs and ideological and political structure of the country as well as to the type and extent of tourism development in the location. Nevertheless, the rationale for government involvement in tourism is based not only on the nature and extent of perceived economic and social benefits of tourism but also on the impracticability or inability of the enterprises, representative organizations or individuals to undertake certain functions (Pearce, 1992). For government intervention to be justified within a market economy environment, there has to be a degree of market failure, a situation where the full costs and benefits of the sector's development are not captured through the price mechanism (Akehurst, Bland and Nevin, 1993). Thus, as Hall and Jenkins (1995) point out, the issue frequently becomes not one of whether government should have a role in tourism development but exactly what that role should be. Current wisdom within developed economies appears to be moving towards a constriction of the role of government and its focus on the area of destination (local or national) marketing with the effect of reducing direct involvement in the HR area.

Clearly, the degree of government involvement in tourism depends on a country's history, socio-economic conditions, the political outlook of the dominant political groupings and the extent to which tourism is already developed (Joppe, 1994). Government intervention can be controlling or supporting of tourism in an active or passive manner. These public interventions can range across the full range of tourism responsibilities and relate to tourism resources, infrastructure, facilities and amenities, distribution channels or, indeed, the tourist. The case for government involvement in the HR aspects of tourism is built, primarily, on the argument that there is a need for tourism to operate with an adequate supply of skilled operative and managerial personnel in order to meet its future personnel needs and to be able to remain competitive in international terms. There is a long-standing acceptance of this role in developed countries although, generally, it is not one that is widely recognized under the umbrella of government involvement in tourism. This is because the role is undertaken within either the education or the employment/training roles that government fulfils across the economy. Public education and training institutions with programmes of education and training for sectors of tourism, notably hotel and catering, date back close to one hundred years, but this public investment in support of the industry has gone relatively unquestioned and with little attempt at objective assessment of its impact.

At a practical level, tourism education, training and development both within the firm and beyond it, as part of public or private institutional provision, is relatively mature in most developed countries and is an evolving area of activity in communities and countries for which tourism and hospitality activity is rather more new. There is, however, ongoing and at times acrimonious debate between providers of tourism and hospitality education and those who see themselves as clients of the system – the industry itself – regarding the relevance, level and focus of education and training (Amoah and Baum, 1997, p. 6).

One of the difficulties for HRM in the context of tourism is that it is expected to dance to the tune of a fragmented and heterogeneous sector where there are few commonly defined needs at a technical or knowledge level. The requirements of major airlines, hotel companies or heritage sites are diverse in themselves but are also significantly different from the needs of SMEs across the sector. The sector also draws in players from areas of activity which may, at best, acknowledge a tenuous association with tourism and, at worst, fail to see their responsibilities in this area at all – such areas can include national parks, leisure and recreational interests, the finance sector, the security services and parts of the retail sector. One of the consequences of a fragmented public and private sector interest in tourism is that there is rarely a clear, single authority with responsibility for the management and direction of HR initiatives in support of the sector. In reality, there is frequently a range of organizations and agencies which have some involvement but also have loyalties and interests that lie outside the domain of tourism and hospitality. Such organizations and providers may include:

- the various industry sub-sectors and their representative associations;
- national, regional or local tourism development agencies (generally public but also in the private domain);
- public sector agencies or government authorities responsible for areas such as heritage, the environment, marine and other water resources, agriculture, national parks etc.;
- national or provincial education providers;
- private education providers;
- specialist training agencies (public and private);
- national employment, labour or manpower agencies and their respective government departments;
- social partner organizations such as trade unions.

What is frequently seen as a practical issue, in that education providers may or may not be delivering appropriate curricula to meet industry's needs, is also an issue of policy concern. In many respects, it is policy shifts that will be required to provide the lead and assist the sector and the wider community in facing up to predicted changes within tourism and hospitality in the future. Amoah's (1998) study is one which seeks to establish the extent to which policy formulation in the area of tourism and hospitality evolves in tandem or in isolation from that applicable within the education, training and development domain. While based on empirical work in western Europe and similar developed country contexts, the findings appear to be considerably more widely applicable. Amoah's study is based on a series of national case studies that were the outcome of local interviews and policy analysis. Amoah postulates that effective linkages between policy formulation and implementation in the tourism and the education/labour market environments are an important building block towards meeting the HR challenges which Spivack (1997) identifies. Amoah argues that this outcome is most effective where specific tourism education policies are articulated and put in place as a result of the convergence of the two supporting policy areas. Amoah has articulated this convergence process through presentation of a conceptual model which places tourism and education/training within a policy conceptual framework (Amoah and Baum, 1997) and identifies some of the key linkages which need to be in place for the effective delivery of tourism education, a delivery that can be fully responsive to the range of future needs identified earlier. This TEP–TEI

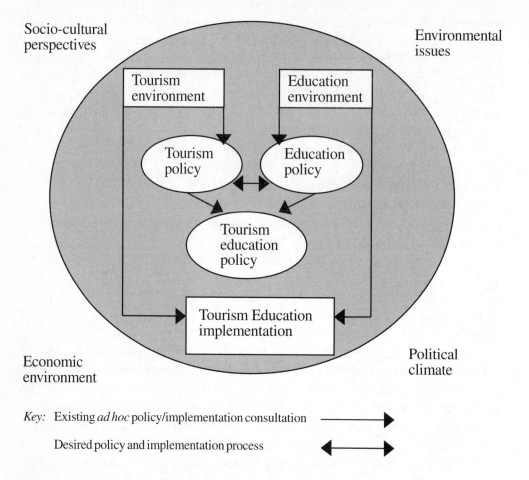

Socio-cultural perspectives

Environmental issues

Economic environment

Political climate

Key: Existing *ad hoc* policy/implementation consultation ⟶

Desired policy and implementation process ⟷

Figure 1.1 Key linkages for effective delivery of tourism education
Source: Amoah and Baum (1977, p. 10)

(Tourism education policy – Tourism education implementation) conceptual framework is represented in Figure 1.1.

In practice, Amoah's research suggests that few if any national or subnational jurisdictions fully acknowledge the policy linkages which the framework proposes. Indeed, the reality in many cases is that the two key policy domains of tourism and education (where both are clearly identifiable) can operate either in virtual isolation or on the basis of dependency and adaptation (where tourism and hospitality are required to respond to or accommodate within policy and practices driven by education and training priorities developed without specific sectoral reference). It is arguable, for example, that the National Vocational Qualification (NVQ), General

National Vocational Qualification (GNVQ) and Scottish Vocational Qualification (SVQ) education framework was developed in the UK in the early 1990s without specific sectoral consideration or recognition of policy priorities within tourism and hospitality. As a consequence, the structural and content focus does not fully meet tourism and hospitality industry needs. That said, it is difficult fully to verify this argument at a policy level because the UK, in common with many jurisdictions, has little more than embryonic components of a national tourism policy.

Tourism, HR and the small business environment

Although there is clear evidence of trends towards globalization of the tourism industry (Go and Pine, 1994), the dominant business model remains that of the small business in most developed and developing countries. However, some recent entrants to the international tourism market-place, such as Singapore, have a preponderance of larger operations in some sectors of the tourism economy, notably accommodation. In the context of this chapter, Morrison's definition of a small business is accepted as one which is:

> financed by one individual or small group, directly managed by its owner(s) in a personalised manner and not through the medium of a formalised management structure. It may or may not be affiliated to an external agency on a continual basis for at least one management function. In comparison to the largest unit of operation within the industry it is perceived as small, in terms of physical facilities, product/service capacity, and number of employees. (1998a, p. 19)

Morrison (1998b) points to the range of sources which indicate that in her sector of interest in particular, that of accommodation, there continues to be a numerical domination by small-scale operations. She reports Sheldon's (1993) study that showed that in excess of 90 per cent of tourist accommodation establishments, world-wide, and that 85 per cent in the UK, are in the small firm category (MSI, 1996). Wanhill (1997) notes a number of key weaknesses in small tourism enterprises, including supply dominated by family businesses; lack of entrepreneurial drive; limited key business skills; and a shortage of financial resources. Morrison (1998a) draws on data from diverse sources in order to gain a picture of the small hotel sector in the UK and her data are presented as Table 1.1. The strategic and operational challenges facing small tourism businesses have important consequences in the area of HRD. Morrison's study points to important HR characteristics of small accommodation operations in terms of employee numbers and family

Table 1.1 Policy and strategy issues of the small hotel firm sector

> - Assets under-utilized by approximately 55 per cent annually
> - Average number of bedrooms per small firm is nine
> - Average number of employees is 50 per cent less than the small firm sector norm
> - Continuing growth in the number of liquidations affecting the small firm
> - Losing market share to large firms and corporate groups
> - Majority operate at the low budget market level in secondary/tertiary locations
> - More sensitive to occupancy and seasonal fluctuations than large firms
> - Profit margins 40 per cent less than corporate-owned, budget-style accommodation
> - Self-employment is 57 per cent higher than the small firm sector norm
> - VAT registration peak (1990) is 22.3 per cent less than the small firm sector norm
> - Volume of UK hotel accommodation is shrinking at the expense of the small firm

Source: Morrison (1998a, p. 191)

ownership. To these can be added a low propensity to train; the impact of seasonality on employment; and the low likelihood of employing skilled staff in key areas.

An important further consideration which impacts upon all tourism businesses but is of particular importance to smaller operations is in the area of marketing, especially destination image marketing. Morrison (1998a) points to the consortia marketing approach as one key strategic response for small businesses, while Buhalis and Main (1998) note the limited impact of technology as an operational or marketing tool in the sector and point to the potential of this vehicle to overcome some of the small business challenges in tourism.

The key point is that tourists engage with a destination through purchases and experiences with a diversity of service providers, from those in the accommodation sector, retail, food service to those in entertainment and local transport. They also experience the destination through other contact with the local community. Each of these contact points is part of what can be called the 'tourism service supply chain' and the overall experience of the visitor is determined by the quality of the service encounter at all or any of these points. It is therefore imperative, from a destination perspective (local or national), that service quality is upheld by all tourism service providers. From a marketing point of view, this imperative justifies public sector investment in HRD within the small businesses of a resort as a means of ensuring a quality experience for all guests. An HR policy or strategy to this effect, therefore, becomes part of a destination's marketing commitment where the benefits, ultimately, are designed to translate into increased visitation and, in particular, enhanced repeat business. This imperative points to one of the strongest justifications for support of an active public sector policy and implementation role of HRD for tourism's small business sector. In terms of practical responses in this regard, Amoah's (1998) research points to approaches at a provincial or regional level (in parts of Canada as well as in Scotland) and at a national level (in the Republic of Ireland) as representative of environments where policy convergence between tourism sector needs and public sector response through HRD is most in evidence and most effectively implemented. These examples are all in environments where small businesses dominate in the tourism sector and where the existence of public sector policies for HRD are greatly influenced by the small business structure of the industry. In these cases, policy convergence is achieved under the auspices of a national or provincial co-ordination agency.

While commencing life as public sector bodies, a number of the Canadian models (for example, the Alberta Tourism Education Council, ATEC) have been moved out of the public sector and now operate as private bodies. The Irish model, through the Council for Education, Recruitment and Training for the Tourism and Hospitality Industry (CERT):

> is unique (in Europe) in that it provides by far the most comprehensive approach to co-ordinating the inputs of education and the tourism industry into a unified system and, through CERT, operates through total co-ordination and the identi-fication of training and development needs at both macro and micro level. (Baum, 1995, p. 207)

The Scottish approach is reflective of a situation where the support for direct state involvement in tourism HRM policy is somewhat more muted than in Ireland but where the benefits for an industry similarly dominated by small businesses are equally evident. The organization of support for tourism HRD is dominated by the public sector in all areas except in-company training and development where there is a combination of public incentives and private implementation. Private tourism education is in fledgling form in Scotland with two initiatives currently at point of start-up. Human resource development for tourism operates at a number of levels in Scotland, all having a measure of public sector involvement. In-company training, while generally a private sector concern, receives public support and encouragement through a variety of generic and tourism-specific initiatives ranging from Investors in People (IiP) to Welcome Host, all of which originate in the public domain. Both Scottish Enterprise and Highlands and Islands Enterprise play a major role in training support and related labour market activities, notably through Tourism Training Scotland (TTS).

The work of agencies such as the Hospitality Training Foundation (HtF) in Scotland, while no longer overtly in the public domain, retains a structure and approach which are greatly informed by thinking from its statutory body days and this is reinforced by its existing status as the National Training Organization (NTO) for tourism. In addition, current employment incentive schemes, within which tourism sector businesses in Scotland actively participate, include a vocational training component. The public policy role is played by the key economic development agencies in Scotland through an active support role with respect to HRD within organizations, offering a range of courses in seasonal locations and promoting specific programmes on a country-wide basis.

Of particular interest, in relation to HR policies for small businesses in tourism, are initiatives which have a strong self-help collaborative focus but for which public agencies play an active 'pump priming' role. Within these, a number of businesses share responsibility, resources and expertise in the interest of a common benefit. Scotland's Hotels of Distinction (a marketing consortium of small businesses) have agreed, with effect from 1998, to the imposition of a training levy on participating members which will be employed to meet the cost of identified training needs within member hotels. Another model is for local collaboration in training, something for which the sector is not noted. The majority of Nairn (north-east Scotland) hoteliers have co-operated to finance and run a Vocational Qualification (VQ) centre in the town for their mutual benefit.

There is no statutory institutional framework for education and training within tourism for Scotland and, as a consequence, considerable fragmentation exists. This fragmentation is addressed through the work of TTS which acts as an umbrella organization working in close association with or on behalf of Scottish Enterprise, Highlands and Islands Enterprise, the Local Enterprise Companies, the Scottish Tourist Board and the private sector. It has, however, limited influence on the work of the universities or other providers operating within the education system. TTS was set up in 1992 under the auspices of the Scottish Tourism Co-ordinating Group. It is a joint industry/public sector forum and was established to lead a new effort to promote effective training and career development in the tourism industry.

Tourism Training Scotland's original strategy, launched in 1993, focused on three key objectives:

- creating a training culture;
- enhancing professional standards;
- improving access to quality training.

Tourism Training Scotland has addressed these objectives through:

- the development of an extensive range of tourism specific courses and materials;
- raising industry awareness of the importance of training through its publications, media activity and participation in industry conferences and events;
- promoting business benefits of effective training and staff development through case studies and the Scottish Thistle Awards, one of which is Student of the Year, sponsored by the Bank of Scotland;
- encouraging uptake of IiP by tourism businesses;
- promoting careers in the tourism industry.

Tourism Training Scotland's programmes have been developed and made available to industry through the Scottish Enterprise and Highlands and Islands Enterprise Networks. The area tourist boards, schools, colleges and universities, and industry associations have also had important roles to play in disseminating the skill message and promoting uptake of the various initiatives. It is possible to tailor these initiatives to the different sectoral needs of, for example, caravan and retail, visitor attractions and art organizations. Each initiative and its focus is presented in Table 1.2.

What these tourism HR policy implementation models have in common is a starting point within identified national and provincial tourism and

Table 1.2 Tourism Training Scotland

Initiative	Focus
• Welcome Host	• basic customer care
• Scotland's Best	• service quality programme
• Natural Cook	• promoting awareness of Scottish produce
• Tourism Business Success	• management skills
• Staff Development Guides	• staff recruitment and development
• Service Quality Guides	• training and advice for tourism retailers
• SVQs	• occupational standards
• Investors in People	• linking skills to business objectives

hospitality policy priorities (not always fully delivered) and the interpretation of these within the context of the HR environment. As a result, modification of the latter is possible and takes place to accommodate sectoral needs. In Ireland, specific tourism and hospitality programmes, operating within different parameters and with divergent objectives from those found in other vocational areas, were developed in the mid-1980s to provide career access within the secondary school system.

This initiative, in turn, influenced the structure and focus of a wider system of vocational provision across other curriculum areas. In other words, tourism and hospitality policy requirements impacted upon and gave direction to wider vocational educational policy within the country. By contrast, in Scotland there appears to be less of a coherent policy co-ordination between tourism and HRD interests, and this is illustrated by the current failure of Scottish tourism education providers to offer significant curriculum inputs in support of two key dimensions of the Scottish tourism marketing thrust, namely activity tourism and cultural/heritage/arts tourism.

CONCLUSION

The international tourism sector is undergoing rapid change. Perhaps the most significant and visible among these changes is the increasing visibility and economic power of the major companies, airlines, hotel chains and theme park operators, which have the ability to employ technological and marketing power in order to gain greater market share. At the same time, their strength poses major challenges for small, independent operators who need to adopt strategies that permit them to remain competitive and, through judicious use of marketing and other alliances, to create positions of specialist strength to ensure their own survival. Operational and marketing considerations are not the only routes necessary for such small businesses to address; those in the HR domain are of equal importance.

There are HR responses which small companies can make on an autonomous basis in order to address possible disadvantages in the labour market. These disadvantages include perceived uncompetitive remuneration and conditions, a limited investment in training and development and limited career opportunities within family-owned organizations. Smaller businesses are also frequently located in more peripheral destinations and this also can increase the challenges which companies face in relation to obtaining, developing and retaining skilled labour. Case study evidence shows that small tourism companies, even when located in remote areas, can compete with the major organizations for the best skills available when they are willing and able to focus fully on this as a concern which impacts upon their market competitiveness. However, the small business sector in tourism in most countries remains relatively immature in its ability to respond competitively to these challenges and, in this context, the role of the public sector can be crucial in ensuring that the destination to which people are going, and its small businesses, can compete effectively. The policy and implementation models from Canada, Ireland and Scotland demonstrate how this can be achieved.

REFERENCES

Akehurst, G., Bland, N. and Nevin, M. (1993), Tourism policies in the European Community member states. *International Journal of Hospitality Management*, **12**, 33–66.

Amoah, V. (1998), Tourism education and training: an exploratory study of links to policy formulation and implementation in the areas of tourism and education. DPhil thesis, University of Buckingham.

Amoah, V. and Baum, T. (1997), Tourism education: policy versus practice. *International Journal of Contemporary Hospitality Management*, **9**(1), 5–12.

Baum, T. (1995), *Managing Human Resources for the European Tourism and Hospitality Industry: A Strategic Approach*. London: Chapman and Hall.

Buhalis, D. and Main, H. (1998), Information technology in peripheral small and medium hospitality enterprises: strategic analysis and critical factors. *International Journal of Contemporary Hospitality Management*, **10**(5), 198–202.

Esichaikul, R. and Baum, T. (1998), The case for government involvement in human resource development: a study of the Thai hotel industry. *Tourism Management*, **19**(4), 359–70.

Go, F. and Pine, R. (1994), *Globalization Strategy in the Hotel Industry*. London: Routledge.

Hall, C. M. and Jenkins, J. M. (1995), *Tourism and Public Policy*. London: Routledge.

Inskeep, E. (1991), *Tourism Planning*. New York: Van Nostrand Reinhold.

Joppe, M. (1994), Government controls on and support for tourism. In S.

Witt and L. Moutinho (eds), *Tourism Marketing and Management Handbook*, 2nd edn. Hemel Hempstead: Prentice Hall.

Market Systems Intelligence (MSI) (1996), *MSI Data Report: Hotels UK*. London: Market Systems Intelligence.

Morrison, A. J. (1998a), Small firm co-operative marketing in a peripheral tourism region. *International Journal of Contemporary Hospitality Management*, **10**(5), 191–7.

Morrison, A. J. (1998b), Small firm statistics: a hotel sector focus. *Service Industries Journal*, **18**(1), 132–42.

Ogden, S. (1998), Comment: benchmarking and best practice in the small hotel sector. *International Journal of Contemporary Hospitality Management*, **10**(5), 189–90.

Pearce, D. (1992), *Tourist Organizations*. Harlow: Longman.

Sheldon, P. (1993), Destination information systems. *Annals of Tourism Research*, **20**(4), 47–70.

Spivack, S. (1997), A consensus model approach for assessing gaps between education system outputs and human resource demands in the tourism and hospitality sector to aid in the attainment of quality service goals. DPhil thesis, University of Buckingham.

Wanhill, S. (1997), Peripheral area tourism: a European perspective. *Progress in Tourism and Hospitality Research*, **3**(1), 47–70.

Wanhill, S. (1998), Tourism in the peripheral areas of Europe. Paper presented at Tourism Research Seminar, Research Centre of Bornholm, Nexø.

CHAPTER TWO

Flexible Labour and Human Resource Management Practices in Small to Medium-sized Enterprises: The Case of the Hotel and Tourism Industry in Australia

Nils Timo and Michael Davidson

INTRODUCTION

The hotel and tourism industry is one of the largest service sectors of the Australian economy and is a major employer of labour. The hotel industry is dominated by a large number of small to medium-sized enterprises (SMEs). The general approach of management shows little commitment to a human resource management (HRM) ideal which views labour as 'human assets'. Rather, the approach is based on treating labour as a cost with management adoption of cost minimization practices. Key features of employment in the industry are low pay, low trade union density, gendered jobs, weak internal labour markets, low skill formation, low levels of HRM professional practices and a reliance on a culture of casualization.

This chapter examines the scope of the SMEs in the hotel industry and examines trends in workplace reform and HRM practice by focusing on four key issues: first, the characteristics of the hotel labour market; second, the trends in HRM practice; third, the implications for labour utilization and service quality; and finally, the implications at policy level.

SMEs in the hotel and tourism industry

No agreed definitions exist of what constitutes small or medium-sized enterprises (SMEs). However, research shows that definitions of small business lack consistency. For example, Burrows and Curran (1989, p. 530) observe that it is 'misleading to talk about a small firm sector where that means there exists some population of firms with a set of characteristics that separates them clearly from other firms in the economy'. Common measurement criteria usually draw upon some unique description or characteristic. A number of permutations and combinations have been used to define SMEs. These include: ownership (self-employed, partnership, proprietary company or constitutional corporation, sole trader, franchise), industry location or sector characteristics (such as manufacture versus services), assets, market share, annual turnover or sales and size of employment.

Data from the Australian Bureau of Statistics (ABS) show that the hotel and tourism industry is predominantly made up of SMEs. Small businesses are defined as having fewer than 19 employees, medium as having between 20 and 99, and large business as having over 100 employees. Of the 21,221 businesses registered, 18,000, or 85 per cent, employed fewer than 20 persons. In relation to the 4,314 registered accommodation establishments (hotels and motels), 3,732, or 87 per cent, employed fewer than 20 employees. While the majority of businesses in the industry can be classified as small businesses, the larger establishments (or 292 large businesses, or 1 per cent) have a greater impact on local economies, accounting for 30 per cent of employment and 32 per cent of gross income (ABS, 1994, Table 4.2).

It is expected that with size of employment comes a range of other factors such as a given level of HRM practice, managerial control systems and management style that develops from a requirement to control labour. In this sense, size of employment allows us to make and test assumptions about managerial practices and the effectiveness of HRM systems. Such an approach is justified when considering the nature of the task in this chapter. The hotel and tourism industry is a large employer of labour. It is often at the forefront of political and policy debates about employment generation at a time when manufacturing has been steadily declining. By studying the employment relations of SMEs in the hotel and tourism industry, we may broaden our understanding of how work is organized, managed and rewarded.

THE HOTEL AND HOSPITALITY INDUSTRY: PROBLEMS OF DEFINITION

There is no strict adherence to definitions of either the tourism or hospitality industries: definitions may vary according to the perspective adopted. The tourism industry is difficult to define precisely because many activities commonly associated with it overlay those of other industries, such as the retail and recreation industries. This diverse and encompassing nature of the industry ensures a significant multiplier effect on local economies. According to the Victorian Department of Labour (1986, p. 23), the range of organizations includes hotels; motels; BYO licensed restaurants (Bring Your Own); restaurants (fully licensed); clubs (fully licensed); caterers, function and convention centres (with and without licence); take-away food outlets (with sit down facilities); cafés (unlicensed); cabarets (licensed); caravan parks; designated tourist attractions and theme parks; travel agencies; and tour and coach operators. This chapter focuses mainly on SMEs in the hotel accommodation sector.

Globalization and competitiveness

On a global scale, tourism has emerged as a significant growth industry and has been increasing at about 7 per cent per annum. Australia has about a 1 per cent share of the total world tourist trade, but, significantly, has over 7 per cent of the world's long-haul trade. The Asia–Pacific region is emerging as having the highest rate of growth in tourism in the world. The expansion of links between airlines, hotels and travel agencies has seen the growth of a global tourism industry unrestrained by national boundaries (Davidson and Faulkner, 1994; Timo, 1996a).

The rapid growth in overseas tourism during the 1980s, especially from Japan and Asia followed by Europe and North America, promoted a surge in building infrastructure such as hotels and resorts, golf courses, and retail establishments. This growth has been mainly financed by overseas investors seeking to capitalize on the growth in domestic real estate prices, or by credit lenders favouring a short term investment. However, the fall in real estate prices and the oversupply of tourism accommodation have meant much of the industry has showed negative returns (ACIRRT, 1996; Davidson and Patiar, 1996). In addition, the currency crisis affecting many Asian economies during late 1997 and early 1998 has reputedly been responsible for a 10 per cent fall in Asian tourists visiting Australia (Anon, 1998).

Competition and product markets

The hotel and tourism product is a diverse mix of services and goods. The product is often difficult to define and measure because it includes a tangible component (such as accommodation, food and beverage, as well as any retail products purchased) and intangibles (such as ambience, décor, service, location, entertainment and leisure facilities). All hotels compete according to a range of criteria such as star grading, niche markets, market segments (holiday or business) and price. Price is usually the key determinant, followed by location. However, the emergence of business tourism (such as conferences) means that the distinctions between different types of tourism establishments become less significant (Timo, 1996a). The product can usually be segmented into family, visitor, business traveller and conventions/exhibitions. Often, tourist accommodation establishments provide a mix of products, for example, motels provide overnight stays for the traveller (whether business or pleasure). In addition, the emergence of ecotourism has seen the growth in destination travel as a key factor where location becomes the product itself.

Productivity and quality issues

Measuring and defining productivity in the hotel and tourism industry present a number of problems. First, productivity lacks an agreed definition and benchmark. Second, productivity and quality are the outcome of both management choice and guest expectations. Third, productivity in services is related to demand and is closely connected to production and consumption (Teare, 1989). Finally, productivity is contingent on a range of factors such as location, characteristics of markets, service/product perishability, characteristics of labour, and consumer expectations. Costs such as bank interest, municipal charges, tax, electricity and supplies are generally fixed, in that a hotel must at least keep itself in readiness irrespective of whether customers are present or not. While hotels are able to adjust room rates to reflect market competition, they are very susceptible to market changes. Many hotels do not make a profit during the first five years of operation (Timo, 1996a). Labour cost is one of the few variables of the tourism production chain that can be varied according to demand. As inventory is a cost, flexible forms of labour are a means to restructure labour use on a 'just-in-time' basis. Labour and productivity are often treated as inseparable when applied to tourism. Hence, it is argued that understanding labour utilization and management practice is essential to understanding how productivity is defined in the hotel and tourism industry.

Merricks and Jones (1986) suggest two ways to improve labour productivity. First, by increasing the performance of individual members of staff through monitoring and re-engineering working practices; second, by restructuring staff into teams and creating a climate for increased staff motivation. Flexible working may also lead to improved productivity. A number of researchers have also linked increased productivity with better reward systems; interpersonal skills training and on-the-job training programmes for managers and staff; efficient design of hotel facilities; and the creation of long term permanent jobs (ACIRRT, 1996; AIC, 1996, for example).

Understanding the current position of hotel productivity in Australia is difficult because of the lack of empirical data on labour costs, competitiveness and productivity. However, a study by the Tourism Task Force entitled *Labour Costs and Training* (1992) was able to estimate productivity using labour costs as a proportion of total payroll. The study indicates that the Australian hotel industry has one of the highest labour cost components as a percentage of revenue at 37.2 per cent, followed by North America (34.7 per cent), continental Europe (31.2 per cent), United Kingdom (28.3 per cent), and Far East/Asia (25.8 per cent). On a proportion of employees per available room, Australia was found to have the second lowest proportion at 0.67, compared to continental Europe, 0.48, followed by North America, 0.68, then United Kingdom, 0.95, and Far East/Asia, 1.16. Despite the higher labour costs, the study found that Australian hotels achieved higher net retail sales/revenue per employee at A$43,932 per employee (second to continental Europe at A$63,379) followed by the United Kingdom, A$43,353, North America, A$41,737, and Far East/Asia, A$28,638. This suggests that Australian hotels have higher productivity per employee (Tourism Task Force, 1992, pp. 13–14). However, despite higher productivity and retail sales/revenue, per room per employee, Australian hotels were found to rank last in terms of hotel gross operating profit. Australian hotels returned 20.4 per cent, as compared to North America, 24.7 per cent, continental Europe, 29.2 per cent, the United Kingdom, 33.9 per cent and Far East/Asia, 34.8 per cent, suggesting that Australian hotel accommodation is less expensive (Tourism Task Force, 1992).

The connection between payment systems and hours of work provided under Australia's centralized system of pay awards has focused on the link between productivity and wages. The Australian Industrial Relations Commission (AIRC) sets wages and conditions that are binding on employers through a system of awards that link hours of work and payment systems. The role of penalty rates (special rates for weekends and late nights) and labour costs features as a major issue in the contemporary debate. Recently, the Australian Hotels Association failed in an attempt to reduce penalty rates on a Saturday and Sunday by 25 per cent. While the hotel industry argued that a reduction in penalty rates would improve employment prospects and make hotels more competitive, the AIRC rejected the claim on the basis that the industry had failed to provide a positive link between penalty rates and employment. It also found that penalty rates were an established feature of the award system and served to bolster take home pay (Penalty Rates Case, The Hospitality Industry – Accommodation, Hotels, Resorts and Gaming Award 1998, 27 March 1998, print no. P9677). Over the last few years there has been a trend by larger hotel employers toward individual enterprise agreements because of changes in employment law. However, the centralized system is still predominant among smaller hotel employers.

CHARACTERISTICS OF THE SME HOTEL AND TOURISM LABOUR MARKET

The Australian hotel and tourism labour market has a number of characteristics that shape the way in which labour is utilized by SMEs. These characteristics often encourage the development of weak internal labour markets and poor HRM practices, and these are discussed below.

Age and seasonal volatility

Work in tourism is integrally linked to the concept of leisure. The rigid boundary between work and leisure becomes blurred as notions of work and play, holidays and fun are intermingled with service and product, promotion and reward. Typically, young people (under 24) dominate the hotel workforce, choosing this type of work for reasons of ease of entry, travel opportunities, variety and friendliness (KPMG Peat Marwick Management Consultants, 1991, pp. 6–7). According to the Tourism Training Australia report (1997), the nature of employment growth into the next century in hotels is expected to be in semi-skilled occupations such as kitchen hands, food attendants, cooks, bar attendants, supervisors, porters and housekeepers. The few skill barriers to jobs in the industry mean that it is often one of the few areas where young people can readily obtain work (Tourism Training Australia, 1997). In addition, low-skilled work has advantages such as perceived favourable interpersonal relations, a convivial social setting and a chance to meet a variety of people including co-workers and guests.

Labour turnover

Labour turnover has a major cost impact on employers, especially SMEs. High turnover represents a loss of skill and experience. The Australian Industry Commission (AIC) estimates the cost of replacing a full-time employee as follows: room attendant (A$4303–5000), waiter (A$4575–5000), chef (A$7197–11,739) and a manager (A$9474–15,884) (AIC, 1996, p. 261, Table 13.13). Industry research suggests that labour turnover is a management problem that can thus be identified and tackled by appropriate managerial action. This includes better recruitment and selection practices, higher wages, more training, career advancement, multi-skilling and worker participation (ACIRRT, 1996).

Labour turnover remains a significant feature of work in the hotel and tourism industry. Reasons given by employees for leaving traditionally include taking up another better paid job within the tourism industry (43 per cent), and moving to another location. The KPMG Peat Marwick survey (1991) also found that 43 per cent of employees who resigned in order to take up another position in the tourism industry did so to further their career, whereas 41 per cent of respondents sought improved wages and conditions. However, for those employees who moved to jobs outside the tourism industry, 58 per cent sought higher wages and conditions and 44 per cent sought to improve their career opportunities. The survey also suggested that the move to jobs outside the industry improved job security, with 47 per cent of respondents seeking employment outside the industry with more secure income and employment (KPMG Peat Marwick Management Consultants, 1991). In addition, many employees hold multiple jobs with up to 25 per cent working in at least one other job. Reasons included seeking to improve take home pay, better jobs and less reliance on one employer as a sole source of income (Timo, 1996a).

Employment size, HRM practice and internal labour markets

According to Jackson (1997), SMEs can be defined by several unfortunate characteristics including 'unprofessional strategy' and HRM practices, inadequate planning and inadequate financial business acumen. Other factors that affect managerial approaches include establishment size, managerial style, ownership (working proprietor or franchisee) and debt/equity. These have implications for the management of labour in SMEs. For example, the size of hotels impacts on the formation of internal labour markets and employment practices. The KMPG Peat Marwick Management Consultants survey (1991) found a significant difference in voluntary resignations between SMEs (employing fewer than 100 employees) and larger hotels (employing more than 100 employees). The survey showed that amongst SMEs, 57.5 per cent of permanent employees resigned during the period June 1989 to June 1990 as opposed to 43.2 per cent for large hotels during the same period.

Trends in labour turnover suggest that labour mobility can be related to inadequate HRM systems. SMEs are less likely to have adequate job descriptions; job policies and procedures; training and development procedures; and grievance procedures that enable employees and their employer to resolve issues without recourse to termination (Nankervis, 1993; Price, 1994). Other management issues identified by industry-based research on SMEs include the following: a lack of well-developed people management skills (particularly amongst supervisory staff); failures in communication with employees; lack of involvement in decision making; lack of training; and a reluctance to make available permanent work (Australian DEET, 1989; KPMG Peat Marwick Management Consultants, 1991 pp. 5–6, 22–7; ACIRRT, 1996; Tourism Training Australia, 1997).

Hotel recruitment and employee performance

SMEs by and large rely on the external labour market for ready skill, rather than using and redeploying existing workers. In this context, there is an absence of well-defined HRM practices in relation to recruitment and selection. This is often due to the absence or relatively low status of the personnel function, or to the owner or operator taking personal charge of recruitment and selection. Advertising, job descriptions, selection, on-the-job training, grievance handling and policy implementation are often *ad hoc*. Often few hotel employees have seen their job description or been aware of an employment manual. Offers of employment are usually made on a casual basis, and this informal job tenure is often a port of entry into permanent employment. Using casual engagements as ports of entry is said to maintain control over staffing levels and to extend more control over employee behaviour and discipline. However, there are costs associated with employing casuals. Hotel management often sees casual employees as being:

- less committed and motivated;
- not as well skilled or trained;
- more prone to higher turnover and multiple jobs holding (reducing their availability).

The above shortcomings are often overlooked in the quest for cheaper labour. In addition, these conditions are often resisted by employees who object to the inherent uncertainty of the relationship. This in turn makes hotel labour markets unstable.

Typically, employment 'strategy' among SMEs is characterized by 'hire and fire' practices (see Johnson, 1981; Bonn and Forbringer, 1992). Thus, a key area for improvement is effective recruitment and selection procedures. Hotels need to expend greater energy on choosing the 'right' person and adopt more widespread compensation and benefits packages in order to retain the right staff. However, industry-wide issues of seasonality, fluctuating demand and product perishability often result in low pay, limited career progression, inadequate rostering and long, often unsocial, working hours.

The importance of numerical flexibility

A central problem of efficiency in the hotel industry is the utilization of capacity in the face of irregular customer/guest arrivals and different levels of demand (over the day, week and season) in operations. Labour in hotels is structured according to forecast demand, and the adaptability in labour costs according to the matching of labour inputs (paid hours) to customer demand. One way of matching labour to demand is by restructuring labour on a just-in-time basis through using numerically flexible forms of labour such as casual workers. Casual employment is usually defined as paid-by-the-hour, hourly engagement with no expectation of additional ongoing work. Timo (1996a) and the AIC (1996) estimate that casual labour comprises 50–70 per cent of employment and that the use of casual employees does not differ significantly between SMEs and larger establishments. Labour needs are structured according to seasonal and diurnal (or irregular) customer demand in the following ways:

- casual staff are used on weekends during peak demand periods and are sent home when demand tapers off;

- salaried (supervisory/managerial) staff are also used at weekends to reduce the effect of penalty rates;
- the number of weekly staff used at weekends or late night is reduced;
- hotel services are rationalized at weekends by closing one or more restaurants and marking used rooms to be cleaned on Monday.

Hotels attempt to link labour and working time arrangements in such a way so as to minimize the cost of labour and paid labour hours (particularly those hours of work attracting a penalty or extra loadings). Working time arrangements are shown in Table 2.1.

Table 2.1 Flexible hotel working time

- Flexible commencing and ceasing times
- Extending the spread of ordinary working hours on any day at single time
- Flexible rostering (notification of roster changes)
- Averaging ordinary hours
- Rearranging penalty or loaded hours to single time (for example, time off in lieu of overtime)
- Changes in the duration of working time
- Restructuring shift arrangements (split shifts, ten-hour and twelve-hour shifts)
- Reduction or elimination of breaks (between periods of work, rest pauses)
- Reducing constraints on managerial discretion regarding the scheduling of work (for example, scheduling of rostered days off (RDOs), breaks, taking of leave)
- Liberalization of restrictions and constraints on use of labour (part-time, casual and seasonal labour)
- Reduction in rostering notice and changing of roster provisions

---

Hotels are able to extend labour flexibility by blurring the distinction between standard and non-standard working hours. Hotels show an ability to mix and match forms of labour with particular working time arrangements, enabling hotels to maintain a supply of labour to match changes in work flow. Ultimately, hotels attempt to use numerical flexibility to unscramble standard and non-standard working hours and to replace these with flexible working time arrangements that reduce the number of paid hours that are, in turn, linked to an employee's employment status (weekly, part time or casual). The extent to which hotels adopt such practices is dependent on a variety of factors. For example, in a hotel whose primary market is stable and where variations in activity levels are minor, the above forms of flexibility may simply not be an issue. However, at the other end of the scale, a small hotel may employ all staff as casuals only when there is demand. Many SMEs insure against a decline in trade by employing all staff as 'permanent' casuals who have regular hours of work each week but who are laid off as soon as demand drops or who are re-engaged at short notice. The feedback from hotel managers suggests that these labour practices are able to achieve payroll savings of 14–16 per cent in terms of paid hours.

A culture of casualization

Can we distinguish a culture of casualization? On the one hand, the reliance on large numbers of casuals may be explained by the seasonal impact on hotels. However, on the other hand, the use of casual labour may also be explained by the strategies employed by hotel and tourism employers to reconstruct labour on a just-in-time basis as part of broader cost minimization and control strategies (Timo, 1996a, 1996b). A casual workforce not only reduces overall labour costs by employing workers on a just-in-time basis. Casualization has become an endemic feature of the industry, often serving as a port of entry to an internal labour market as well as a useful mechanism for allocating initial training to employees without the risks associated with full-time employment. Casualization enables employers to see whether an employee 'works out' in a form of probationary employment, and this reduces the risks associated with putting a person on permanent and running foul of unfair dismissal laws. For employees, the higher penalty rate associated with casualization (20–25 per cent under hospitality and tourism awards) enables employees to maximize their income, maintain multiple job holding and minimize dependence on any one employer for their livelihood (Timo, 1996a, 1996b).

Flexible labour and skill formation

Flexible labour and turnover may have advantages for hotel employers by reducing training costs and facilitating skills acquisition (Bowey, 1976). However, the use of flexible labour creates a conundrum for hotel managers. On the one hand, turnover is construed as a negative factor contributing to casualization and high turnover cost; engendering lack of motivation; and being detrimental to the hotel in terms of standardization and service quality. On the other hand, turnover has positive effects. It is argued to be a necessary feature of hotel work by allowing hotels a degree of flexibility in staffing; and by ensuring an infusion of new 'fresh faces' in order to maximize favourable guest reactions. It is also considered an integral mechanism for skill acquisition in employees. For SMEs, turnover can vary from 30 to 300 per cent. Average job tenure is three to six months, with the high average around eighteen months. Highest levels of turnover are usually found in food and beverage and kitchen, with the lowest in administration and front office.

Typically SMEs offer employees little opportunity for new skill acquisition and upward career mobility. Thus labour turnover and skill formation are linked: for example, promotional opportunities in SMEs are often limited. Changing employment (usually by moving to another organization) becomes the only viable method of acquiring further skill and career development. Many hotel employees view long-term employment in the industry as a career objective; however, few remain with their current employer beyond twelve months. The external labour market becomes a significant mechanism for allocating skill. Workers employed in the industry for an extended time are likely to acquire significant on-the-job skills. The overall pattern of skill acquisition and job mobility in the hotels studied is consistent with the concept of acquiring skills and competencies through a series of changes in employment in the industry, as opposed to remaining with one or a few hotel employers during one's working life. Alternatively, this work is viewed simply as a job until one has a 'real job' outside of the industry.

Wages, training and skills

The skill and qualifications profile of the hotel and tourism industry shows that the industry is both labour intensive and low skilled. In terms of education, only 11 per cent of employees had a recognized trade qualification as compared to an all industries average of 16.4 per cent. In addition, 70.6 per cent of employees had no post-school qualifications, as compared to 52.9 per cent for all industries, according to the AIC (1996, p. 257).

Low levels of skill are connected with low pay; hotel and tourism workers are generally low paid. Real average hourly earnings for all non-managerial hotel and tourism employees are lower than the all industry average for Australian workers for the period 1980–90. This position has worsened during the last decade. For example, workers in the industry on average earn only 73–86 per cent of the all industry average (AIC, 1996; Timo, 1996a). Average weekly earnings for employees in hotels and tourism in 1996 were A$347.40 as compared to an all industry average of

A\$536.80 (Australian Bureau of Statistics, 1995, Tables 6 and 7; Australian Bureau of Statistics, 1997, Tables 6.3 and 6.6).

Management, HRM practice and informal rule-making

Often in SMEs, a strong individualism and a paternalistic approach underlie hotel management's relationship with employees. This control enables a range of informal work practices to occur at department level between the manager/supervisor and the individual employee. The distribution of rewards and favours according to this informal system of individual bargaining (e.g. access to paid overtime, more favourable rosters, training, and days off) goes on all the time and illustrates how the hotel workplace is a site of significant conflict and power relationships. Allocation of these 'rewards' also engenders employee loyalty and commitment to the department (or alternatively encourages 'exit' behaviour). Workers may internalize the organizational values of the workplace (Croney, 1988). This point is crucial in understanding how labour use strategies are determined, and why existing managerial practices go largely unchallenged.

There is an absence of clearly defined routes to managerial and supervisory positions in the industry. People begin hotel management careers from a range of different points of entry, including departments of food and beverage, catering and banqueting, or marketing and sales. Experience in a major revenue earning/income department is considered essential for promotion. Similarly, for operational staff such experience is not limited to a single hotel, but acquired through multiple job holding across a range of establishments. Mobility is a crucial feature of hotel management career development. At each stage of a manager's career, the emphasis is on task performance and technical understanding. In this way, hotel management is also very much 'hands-on'.

The absence of a craft tradition encourages a form of 'active crisis' management (see Dann, 1990). Benson and Worland (1992) suggest that the culture of hotel management engenders visible management styles where the emphasis is on a 'being there' style of managing rather than on achievement of results. This is encouraged by the nature of hotel management work that encourages managers to respond to problems by being downwardly mobile. Having dealt with the immediate problem, however, the manager does not pause to analyse the problem but passes on to the next operational crisis. The hotel culture reinforces this activity-based behaviour as the 'right way of getting the job done' and will reward it with praise and career progression. According to Wood (1992), 'being there' styles of management give rise to procedures characterized by informality of communication between management and staff, in conjunction with a paternalistic and authoritarian approach. On the issue of paternalism/authoritarianism, Guerrier and Lockwood (1989) found that managers saw the development and care of their staff as a central part of their role, but noted that they did little to convert this into direct action, except where participation was management-led to meet specific ends. In the case of owner/operators, the notion of ownership of the business defines the extent of paternalism in the way that employees are treated. The above managerial style also encourages informal rule-making. Surveys of workplace agreements show that, in general, SMEs manage flexibility through informal workplace agreements with employees, with only 10 per cent of small employers opting for formal workplace agreements (ADIR, 1996 pp. 55–6). It is at the level of the individual work unit that informal working arrangements occur.

There are two forms of informal arrangements found. The first involves arrangements directly between employees themselves in terms of changing rosters or banking of hours as agreed between employees. This informal arrangement between employees is generally based on reciprocity and is often associated with sharing shifts in order to maximize leisure time. The second involves arrangement between supervisor and employee. This could involve coming to a private arrangement with a supervisor in order to gain some advantage (for example, time off when needed or access to more work). Most employees recognize these informal arrangements, but are often not prepared to complain about their impact upon employment entitlements. (Complaints usually happen after one has left the service of the employer.) Another difficulty in assessing the consensual or arbitrary nature of informal working-time arrangements in SMEs is that the time preferences of employees have become increasingly diversified. Female employees interviewed tended to prefer flexible starting/ceasing times that coincided with family commitments, whereas male workers prefer blocks of working time to maximize leisure time.

The nature of turnover, the highly casualized nature of the labour market and paternalistic managerial attitudes mean that many SMEs in the hotel industry have low levels of unionization. Union membership in hotels varies according to location and existing union presence, varying from 1.75 per cent in high tourism areas such as Australia's Gold Coast, to 12 per cent in central business districts (Timo, 1996a).

Good employee relations and service quality

The relationship between HRM practices and service quality is becoming increasingly recognized. Utilization of good employee relations in small companies can be affected by various factors, such as size, values and rewards. The smaller the number of employees, the greater the opportunity exists for more effective personal working relationships through the use of direct management motivation and encouragement. The use of support and intrinsic values has been noted by Mullins (1996) who put forward three broad categories of motivation for employees. These relate to the provision of economic rewards; intrinsic satisfaction such as positive feedback and self-esteem; and involvement in decision-making. Cultural climate and a quality-first ethos are important for service organizations. Customer perceptions of what is quality and value for money are the yardstick by which a business will be judged as successful or not.

According to Davidson (1998), effective organizational climates are connected to notions of equity. To date, however, many SMEs do not understand this linkage. In a study of organizational climate among hotel employees in south-east Queensland, Davidson found that the single biggest dissatisfaction factor in the employment relationship was the perceived unfairness of the reward process and lack of equity in treatment. This places considerable importance on effective reward policies and grievance procedures. Functional flexibility is also inextricably linked with service quality. Some SMEs are now process based rather than being solely function based. For example, in a process-based hotel, one employee will not only check in the guest and take luggage to the room but also service the room, provide simple in-room dining and give information about other recreational/leisure services (Davidson and DeMarco, 1999). These forms of work re-organization rely on effective training systems. In the Australian context, the issue of flexibility has been linked with deregulation of wages by the introduction of workplace agreements. Many agreements have inserted training provisions. However, these training provisions encourage more work from fewer employees rather than genuine skill development.

DISCUSSION: LABOUR UTILIZATION AND HRM PRACTICES IN SME HOTELS

This chapter has argued that SMEs in the hotel and tourism industry have adopted particular approaches to labour utilization and the organization of work. The labour market is predominantly young, gendered, highly mobile and low paid. Hotels are dependent on a numerically flexible and casualized workforce. The chapter identified a range of flexible measures associated with numerically flexible labour practices and flexible working-time arrangements. What does this say about the management of SMEs? First, they have been successful in trading off functional flexibility through the widespread use of numerical flexibility. Second, the use of working-time flexibility has replaced traditional concepts of 'standard' working hours. Numerical flexibility and working-time flexibility often operate in tandem in order to meet variability in demand. Increases in work flow are met by numerically flexible workers connected to flexible working-time practices.

The volatile nature of work in hotels contributes to a culture of casualization. Casualization serves a function of reducing costs for SMEs. Labour costs are connected to payment systems that in turn are linked to working time. Labour is a major cost in an industry dominated by contingent demand. In this way, labour can be purchased on a just-in-time basis, without the need to tie up capital in human inventory in the form of full-time or regular commitment to provide work. Driving down labour costs through treating labour on a just-in-time basis is seen as an important factor in competitiveness. Casual employment can also serve as a port of entry to the core workforce by serving as a filter for screening employees. There are clear productivity benefits for hotel management arising from these forms of work organization. These are reducing labour costs and lessening reliance on core employment to supply necessary skills. Under such conditions, internal labour markets become difficult to construct; unsystematic HRM practices in turn perpetuate this weakness.

According to Price (1994), smallness and isolation have shielded HRM practices and managerial attitudes from critical analysis by a wider audience. The lack of commitment to the widespread implementation of well-defined payment structures and systems and training and career development, and the failure to use more sophisticated HRM practices is typical of many low pay and low skill industries. The basic long-term goals of HRM practices in SMEs are contingent upon a broader short-term opportunistic business strategy of minimizing labour costs.

The way forward

There are two choices facing SMEs and the hotel industry generally. Management can continue to accept a labour market model that sees the way forward in terms of increasingly numerically flexible, low-paid casualized workers with limited access to training and careers, and that affords hotels a competitive edge based on price rather than quality. Or, alternatively, management can attempt to move towards a model of employment relations and competitive advantage driven by quality, and by a more skilled and motivated, better paid and more stable workforce. This can be achieved by undertaking a number of HRM activities as suggested below:

- solutions to labour turnover must have regard to the job search strategies of both hotel management and the employees that they supervise;
- current managerial practices that contribute to labour instability and engender weak internal labour markets should be replaced by more planned and determined HRM practices that aim for labour retention through value adding and training;
- reducing turnover requires hotel management to adopt a more integrated approach encompassing recruitment, selection and employment relations practices such as job descriptions, job design, training and career planning, skills development, better pay systems (based on seniority), and better supervisory training;
- there should be greater employee participation in work planning, rostering and hours of work choices;
- a quality-first approach should be adopted by linking skills development to quality enhancement;
- better staff planning could be introduced in order to minimize effects of contingent demand;
- broad-based multi-skilling training strategies could be introduced;
- finally, there needs to be a shift in strategies concerned with achieving greater control over labour utilization towards strategies and practices that aim for greater control over labour retention.

Acknowledgements

The help of officers and staff of the Australian Centre for Industrial Relations Research and Teaching (ACIRRT); the Australian Workers Union of Employees, Queensland; the Queensland Hotels Association; the Queensland Motel and Accommodation Association; Taryn Kerr, Mike Salinos,

Elizabeth Noble, Sandy Powie; and managers and staff of the hotels studied is greatly appreciated.

REFERENCES

Anon. (1998), *Australian*, 21 February, Sydney.

Australian Bureau of Statistics (ABS) (1994), *Hospitality Industries Australia, 1991–1992*, Catalogue No. 8674.0. Canberra: AGPS.

Australian Bureau of Statistics (ABS) (1995), *Labour Costs Australia 1993–1994*, Catalogue No. 6348.0. Canberra: AGPS.

Australian Bureau of Statistics (ABS) (1997), *Labour Statistics Australia 1997*, Catalogue No. 6101.0. Canberra: AGPS.

Australian Centre for Industrial Relations Research and Training (ACIRRT) (1996), *Casual Workers, Employment Security and Economic Competitiveness in the Australian Hospitality Industry: Recent Developments and Implications for Policy*. Sydney: ACIRRT, University of Sydney.

Australian Department of Employment, Education and Training (DEET), Women's Bureau (1989), *New Brooms: Restructuring Issues for Women in the Service Sector*. Canberra: AGPS, pp. 110–84.

Australian Department of Industrial Relations (ADIR) (1996), *Annual Report 1995: Enterprise Bargaining in Australia*. Canberra: AGPS.

Australian Industry Commission (AIC) (1996), *Tourism Accommodation and Training*. Report No. 50. Melbourne: AGPS.

Benson, T. and Worland, D. (1992), Hotel international. In R. Lansbury and D. Macdonald (eds), *Workplace Industrial Relations: Australian Case Studies*. Melbourne: Oxford University Press, pp. 96–125.

Bonn, M. and Forbringer, L. (1992), Reducing turnover in the hospitality industry: an overview of recruitment selection and retention. *International Journal of Hospitality Management*, **11**(1), 47–63.

Bowey, A. (1976), *The Sociology of Organisations*. London: Maddern & Stroughton.

Burrows, R. and Curran, J. (1989), Sociology research on service sector small businesses: some critical conceptual considerations. *Work, Employment and Society*, **3**(4), 527–39.

Croney, P. (1988), *An investigation into the management of labour in the hotel industry*. MA thesis, University of Warwick.

Dann, D. (1990), The nature of managerial work in the hospitality industry. *International Journal of Hospitality Management*, **9**(4), 319–34.

Davidson, M. (1998), *Organisational climate of south-east Queensland hotels*. Unpublished research, Griffith University, Gold Coast.

Davidson, M. and DeMarco, L. (1999), Corporate change: education as a catalyst. *International Journal of Contemporary Hospitality Management*, **11**(1).

Davidson, M. and Faulkner, W. (1994), Issues and challenges in tourism research and education. *Tourism Management*, **15**(5), 390–3.

Davidson, M. and Patiar, A. (1996), *Hospitality education: a critical success factor for emerging tourism destinations*. Paper presented at Indo-Australian Symposium on Tourism, Culture and Hospitality, University of Madras.

Guerrier, Y. and Lockwood, A. (1989), Developing hotel managers – reappraisal. *International Tourism and Hospitality Management*, **8**(2), 82–9.

Jackson, S. (1997), Mistakes likely to be fatal for SMEs. *Australian*, 13 October, p. 33.

Johnson, K. (1981), Towards an understanding of labour turnover. *Service Industries Review*, **1**(1), 4–17.

KPMG Peat Marwick Management Consultants (1991), *The Tourism Labour Market – Constraints and Attitudes Report*. Prepared for Tourism Training Australia, Sydney.

Merricks, P. and Jones, P. (1986), *The Management of Catering Operations*. London: Holt, Reinhardt and Winston.

Mullins, L. (1996), *Management and Organisational Behaviour*, 4th edn. London: Pitman.

Nankervis, A. (1993), *Productivity Service Excellence and Innovation in South East Asian Hotels*. Sydney: Department of Employment Relations, University of Western Sydney (Nepean).

Price, L. (1994), Poor personnel practice in the hotel and catering industry: does it matter? *Human Resource Management Journal*, **4**(4), 44–62.

Teare, R. (1989), The hospitality industry in the 1990s: some critical developments. *Marketing Intelligence and Planning*, **7**(9/10), 48–9.

Timo, N. (1996a), *Employment relations and management in the hotel and tourism industry.* Case studies PhD, University of Southern Queensland, Toowoomba.

Timo, N. (1996b), Staff turnover in hotels. *Labour Economics and Productivity,* 8(1), 43–81.

Tourism Task Force (1992), *Labour Costs and Training.* Sydney: Tourism Task Force.

Tourism Training Australia (1997), *Workforce 2020.* Canberra: Australian National Training Authority.

Victorian Department of Labour (1986), *Report of the Training Needs into the Victorian Tourism and Hospitality Industry,* December. Melbourne: Department of Labour.

Wood, R. (1992), *Working in Hotels and Catering.* London: Routledge.

CHAPTER THREE

Creating and Maintaining a Competitive Advantage

Jay Kandampully

INTRODUCTION

The rapid growth of tourism into a global industry and its transformation towards maturity have presented new challenges for the managers of hospitality, tourism and leisure small to medium-sized enterprises (SMEs). The World Tourism Organisation (1991) forecasts continued growth for the tourism industry beyond the year 2000. The turn of the century has forced managers to confront the prospect of an ever-growing intensity of competition and a continuous increase in customer expectations. Relentless advances in technology create products and services with ever shorter life cycles and, hence, diminished customer appeal. Products and services deemed satisfactory by the customer today will undoubtedly prove unsatisfactory to the same customer tomorrow. Managers have realized that traditional approaches to management are inadequate in keeping abreast with an escalating competitive market. To differentiate their product and maintain market leadership, managers will need to adopt approaches which effect improvement and innovation of the organization's systems, procedures and people. In labour-intensive service industries, it may be argued that the human factor holds the ultimate balance in the organization's success because of the important interaction between employees and customers at the service interface. If SMEs are to enhance the effectiveness of the human factor it is imperative that they address the strategies and concepts adopted by leading service organizations. Clearly, not all will be fully appropriate in SMEs for reasons such as organization size; employee role specialization; limited financial resources; and significant seasonal demand fluctuations. However, concepts of service quality provision remain fundamental, irrespective of an organization's size, for the creation and maintenance of competitive advantage.

The ability to offer a superior quality of service has been recognized as the most effective means of ensuring that a company is able to distinguish its offering from the comparable offerings of its competitors (Zeithaml, Berry and Parasuraman, 1996). Buzzell and Gale (1987) find that companies offering superior service achieve higher than normal growth in market share. Furthermore, an organization's ability to offer superior service constitutes a weapon both unique and consistently available (Berry, Parasuraman and Zeithaml, 1988). This will allow the organization to develop a strength which is difficult for their competition to duplicate. It has become increasingly important for firms to offer superior service and to exceed customer expectations (Wren, 1988; Berry and Parasuraman, 1991), delighting customers as opposed to merely satisfying their needs. In service organizations, managers need to understand that customers will judge quality according to the performance of employees because first impressions are important and workers embody the 'quality orientation' of the organization's culture. In order to offer a matchless level of service, leading service organizations have moved away from the traditional management concepts (Peters, 1989). Given the present trends, hotel, tourism and leisure services must develop creative strategies to ensure that one-time customers are transformed into loyal and satisfied repeat guests who act as the firm's most effective marketing executives.

This chapter provides an overview of service quality considerations essential for the creation and maintenance of competitive advantage in hospitality, tourism and leisure SMEs. It does this by introducing the notion of service challenges and then focuses on some common ways of meeting these challenges.

Service challenges

The superiority of leading service organizations may be attributed to their ability in augmenting existing service quality on a continuous basis. From a customer's perspective, it is the service element (post-sales service and customer–employee interaction in a service interface) that effectively increases the value of an organization's product/service offering. Moreover, in the tourism and hospitality industry, products and services cannot be sold in isolation. Commonly they are offered in combination; not only does one support the other, but it is this combination that significantly increases the value to the customer. Services are 'intangible' because the customer does not receive product ownership nor can services be patented; hence they are not predisposed to duplication. In the last two decades there has been increased global competition. Managers recognize that the provision of superior service is a formidable strategic challenge for hospitality, tourism and leisure SMEs if they are to maintain success and increased customer loyalty, thereby ensuring long-term success (Zeithaml and Bitner, 1996).

While service organizations aim to gain customers' loyalty, customers, on the other hand, seek an organization's service loyalty (the assurance of a consistent and superior quality of service) as proof of the organization's commitment to offering superior service, both in the present and for the long term. In a competitive market service loyalty should precede customer loyalty so that SMEs can convince customers of their commitment to superior quality of service. In other words, future success will be determined by the organization's ability to offer service loyalty, which means fulfilling customers' present and future needs. An effective way to achieve this is by enabling service personnel to offer exceptional service. This requires them to operate cross-functionally: for example, a receptionist may adopt responsibility for more than simply checking-in clients. In other words, operations in SMEs should focus on 'process' issues rather than 'task' issues. Typically, in SMEs this means training employees to be multi-skilled (the ability to work in more than one department and to undertake more than one job). This concept promotes flexibility and engenders employee commitment to and ownership of the services they offer. Much contemporary management literature supports the view that newer concepts focusing upon process issues are essential for creating and maintaining competitive advantage. Some of the concepts most commonly cited are:

- service empowerment;
- service recovery;
- service guarantee;
- service inter-relationships;
- service loyalty.

Practising service empowerment

Every thing you are against weakens you; every thing you are for empowers you

Empowerment is when an organization encourages and commonly rewards its employees for exercising initiative in every aspect of their day-to-day work. In an organization, rigid policies, structures and systems often act as barriers to individual employees' talent and imagination. Moreover, this framework prohibits an organization from reaping the full potential of its human resources. The concept of empowerment allows an organization to use its employees more effectively, while benefiting the customers and the organization.

The guiding philosophy of empowerment is non-bureaucratic and oriented towards the worker. The employee-empowerment approach to service is considered one of the best options available to service managers when dealing with problems of customer complaint and operational bottle-necks. This may be especially useful given the peaks and troughs of customer demand and employee work schedules in hospitality, tourism and leisure SMEs. Empowering service employees facilitates a rapid response to customers' needs. This enhances the quality of service and has the potential to lower operational and administrative costs.

Management literature proposes the oldest and long-standing *control-oriented* model and the newly recognized *involvement-oriented* model to lead service organizations. While the former is often referred to as the top–down, bureaucratic and mechanistic management style, the latter has been described as the commitment approach, but is more often referred to as the involvement-oriented empowerment approach to service. The management philosophy on which the involvement model is developed is the crucial differentiating factor between the two approaches. It assumes that all members of an organization's hierarchy possess the capacity to think, co-ordinate and control their own immediate working environment. Lawler (1992) argues that the involvement model is superior due to its direct effect on four organizational performance variables: cost and productivity, quality, speed in responding to customer requests, and innovation.

According to Zemke and Schaaf (1989) empowerment consists of an organizational element and a personal element. The former encourages employees to work creatively in the customer's best interests. In this instance management has the responsibility of providing employee support. Workers in these situations need to be rewarded appropriately. Management's effectiveness lies in developing tactics which convince front-line workers they are empowered to work for the customer. Empowerment may therefore be viewed as a process of realizing employees' full potential by minimizing bureaucratic constraints which prevent creativity.

Hospitality, tourism and leisure SMEs must attract, nurture and develop employees through appropriate selection and recruitment processes and then through training designed to develop their capacity and potential. Empowerment is the next step beyond simply training employees to undertake systematized tasks according to procedures. It is a means of encouraging and rewarding employees' successes and tolerating their mistakes when well-intended efforts fail.

Service recovery

Contemporary management literature attributes a firm's competitive advantage to its capability or core competencies (Prahalad and Hamel, 1990). The human element plays a key role in the service and consumption process. However, despite efforts to minimize error, mistakes are often unavoidable. Researchers have demonstrated that breaking the service promise is the single most important way in which service companies fail their customers (Berry, Zeithaml and Parasuraman, 1990).

Service recovery is a systematic service process undertaken by an organization in an effort to return aggrieved customers to a state of satisfaction after a service or product has failed to live up to expectations. Most customers are sympathetic to the unforeseen service failures which may occur despite a service provider's commitment to offer superior service. Indeed, customers frequently assist in solving the problems caused by service failures. Surprisingly, customers seldom seem unhappy about service mishaps except when the service organization is unwilling to claim responsibility for the mishap, and when the service provider is unable to undertake immediate action to recover the failed service. From a customer's perspective, recovering a failed service helps reassure them that an efficient and quality service will be maintained. This may be achieved by:

- prejudging failure-prone points in the service system using techniques of mapping, flow-charting, work study, critical incident analysis (blueprinting) and establishing emergency service support. For example, the check-in and check-out times in a hotel reception during group arrivals and departures frequently constitute a failure-prone area. Blueprinting enables service managers to visually recognize and establish possible fail-points and determine the means by which bottle-neck areas can be supported;
- training service personnel with the skills and techniques necessary to offer customers a conscious service of recovery. Service personnel need to know not only *how* they can offer services to recover from a failed service situation, but how this service should be *conducted*: customers should be properly informed of the situation; an apology made for the inconvenience; and an explanation provided, detailing the actions being taken to rectify the issue;
- service empowerment, which is one of the aspects most pertinent to a service personnel's ability to act in recovery situations. In many service failure situations, the service personnel, although capable of undertaking

immediate recovery, are not permitted to do so since they may not have the authority to take action deemed beyond their prescribed job task. Only through empowerment are service personnel offered the opportunity of initiating action without prior consultation. This reduces the lead time between complaint and resolution, helping to reduce the 'severity' of the problem.

Services may fail at critical points along the delivery process. If this happens, organizations need a recovery strategy to help regain the customer's trust. Compensation for the inconvenience confirms the organization's acceptance of responsibility for service failure. It is possible to turn a failed service into a positive advantage. The fact that something has gone wrong presents an opportunity to show the customer how much his or her patronage is valued. However, the success of the service of recovery is dependent on demonstrable empathy with the customer. The concept of service recovery provides service personnel with the possibility of immediate corrective action when something goes wrong and the opportunity to eliminate future failures.

Service guarantees

In any business encounter, one side of the transaction is always being asked to assume all or more of the risk than the other

Services are typically intangible and cannot be reworked or returned; the customer makes a purchase in the trust and expectation of receiving a 'good' result. Hence, when service customers purchase a service (unable to see or pre-test the outcome), they take a higher risk than the service providers. In hospitality, tourism and leisure SMEs, managers need to acknowledge and use that opportunity to achieve competitive advantage. They should seek to create risk-free transactions so that the organization is able to attract and positively influence prospective customers who may wish to sample or avail themselves of the organization's services. A risk-free service transaction will be seen by an SME's prospective customer as a bonus, adding value to the result that he or she wishes to achieve. A service guarantee should assure the customer of service reliability. Additionally, service guarantees enhance a number of important issues such as immediate customer feed-back; identification of 'fail-points'; customer satisfaction; employee performance, a service-oriented culture and competitiveness in the market-place. A number of researchers (see Berry et al., 1990; Parasuraman, Berry and Zeithaml, 1991) conclude that a guarantee of reliability is at the heart of excellent service; it constitutes the single most important factor for most customers.

Once service guarantees are established they provide the management team with customer-related information to plan, anticipate changes in the market-place and respond to changes more quickly than their competitors. A service guarantee is a double-barrelled device for improvement – informing customers what to expect and ensuring that the services delivered meet an agreed standard. A guarantee reinforces the service promise of an organization to its customers and has the potential to positively influence buying behaviour. A service guarantee also enables SMEs to learn quickly about customers' expectations and react accordingly, converting dissatisfied customers into satisfied customers. Above all, customers seem to appreciate the guarantee, since the commitment to service the guarantee shows an organization's trust in customers which makes them feel valued. Service guarantees can help create a service driven by customers. A knowledge of customers' expectations and how to satisfy them creates resonance between purchaser and supplier. Service guarantees set criteria for customers; they also dictate the standard to which an organization needs to train its workers, thereby ensuring that the company will be able to deliver a premium quality service (Maher, 1991).

Service interrelationships

Services in hospitality and tourism SMEs are produced, offered, consumed and perceived in an interrelational manner. The prosperity of service organizations is determined by the degree to which management is able to develop and nurture interdependent relationships. Almost all business interactions may be conceived as relationships between firms and customers. For example, customer relationships with the firm may be viewed as business interactions; customer relationships with employees become an effect of direct contact during service delivery; and customer relationships with suppliers occur where the supplier is an intermediary such as a tour operator.

For customers, service personnel in hospitality and tourism SMEs represent the organization, since customers tend to maintain close relationships with these employees. It is useful to view these associations as: employee relationships with the firm which benefit from each other's growth; employee relationships with customers where employees develop close relationships with customers which often supersede their allegiance to the firm; and employee relationships with shareholders where workers are encouraged to own company shares.

Future organizational growth is dictated by the SME's ability to extend its relationships to all 'partners' including suppliers and shareholders. One of the main functions of marketing activities in services is to enhance, maintain and strengthen these relationships. The growth and prosperity of hospitality and tourism SMEs are dependent on their co-existence and growth. Every business has a vested interest in maintaining a good relationship with suppliers. Small to medium-sized enterprises are usually supplied with materials and customers; for example, in hotels, suppliers may undertake to offer food materials or cleaning materials and travel agents may supply hotels with customers. However, most SMEs are family-owned ('private limited companies') and so the significance of shareholder relationships is less important than would be the case for large hospitality and tourism organizations.

Service loyalty

Delivering superior service quality has been recognized as the most effective means of ensuring a company's success

Customer perception of service quality is based on the degree of similarity between expectations and experience. Where comparability is apparent customers are deemed to be satisfied. However, in many cases, this will not create a competitive advantage because customer expectations must be exceeded rather than simply being satisfied. Customers will remain loyal to a service organization if the value of what they receive is determined to be relatively greater than that expected from competitors (Zeithaml and Bitner, 1996). While service quality may be considered essential in convincing customers to choose one service organization over another, many organizations have realized that maintaining excellence on a consistent basis is imperative if they are to gain customer loyalty. This perspective has created a shift in orienting service strategy towards a 'service promise'. According to Parasuraman *et al.*, 1991, customers desire continuing close relationships with service providers. Therefore, it is important for SMEs to conceptualize the service concept beyond short-term financial satisfaction. Customer satisfaction no longer constitutes the convincing focus for success. In today's competitive environment, customers' expectations and technological innovation demand that service leaders distinguish themselves from the competition by exceeding customer expectations.

Customers' perception of exceptional service is often associated with the personal interaction of the employees. Services management literature has repeatedly emphasized the importance of the human element in the delivery of superior service (Parasuraman, Zeithaml and Berry, 1985; Solomon, Surprenanat, Czepiel and Gutman, 1985; Crosby and Stephens, 1987; Gronroos, 1990). Moreover, the human propensity for the delivery of superior service is greatly enhanced by continuous service innovation. Indeed, technological implementation and the subsequent changes in the service process not only have the potential to positively affect employee–customer interaction, but may actually augment the importance of the human element as an organization's competitive edge.

CONCLUSION

Service excellence may be considered an integral part of any superior service (Berry and Parasuraman, 1992), rather than simply a value-adding component. This repositioning of the 'quality' element of service provision has major ramifications for managers of SMEs, and they must reconsider and redesign their service.

We live in a service economy where relationships are becoming increasingly important in terms of our business and personal lives. Customer satisfaction and subsequent desire to develop a relationship emanate from the emotional connection to the service provider. In many services, emotion is a significant element that shapes customer perception of quality and leads the customer to buy from a particular service provider. Customer loyalty and trust are gained by the provision of seamless, consistent and superior service. While customer services aim to satisfy the expressed needs of the customer, service loyalty enables the firm to understand and anticipate expressed needs. Effective anticipation requires that service consistently remains one step ahead of customer needs. It is apparent that products and services should be provided before the need has been identified by the customer; services cannot be deemed superior if they become evident only upon request. If customer trust is absent there is no foundation for a permanent and successful relationship, and hence no loyalty. Thus, service loyalty is a prerequisite in a competitive environment if an organization is to create and maintain competitive advantage. It is through service loyalty that an organization achieves customer satisfaction and willingness to participate in the relationship. While service organizations aim to gain customers' loyalty, customers, on the other hand, seek an organization's service loyalty (the assurance of a consistent and superior quality of service) as proof of the organization's commitment to offering superior service, both in the present and the long term. This concept is based on the premise that service loyalty precedes customer loyalty.

REFERENCES

Berry, L. L. and Parasuraman, A. (1991), *Marketing Services: Competing Through Quality*. New York: Free Press, pp. 55–73.

Berry, L. L. and Parasuraman, A. (1992), Prescriptions for a service quality revolution in America. *Organisational Dynamics*, Spring, 5–15.

Berry, L. L., Parasuraman, A. and Zeithaml, V. A. (1988), The service quality puzzle. *Business Horizon*, September–October, 35–43.

Berry, L. L., Zeithaml, V. A. and Parasuraman, A. (1990), Five imperatives for improving service quality. *Sloan Management Review*, Summer, 29–38.

Buzzell, R. D. and Gale, B. T. (1987), *The PIMS Principles. Linking Strategy to Performance*. New York: Free Press.

Crosby, L. A. and Stephens, N. (1987), Effects of relationship marketing on satisfaction, retention, and prices in the life insurance industry. *Journal of Marketing Research*, **24**, November, 404–11.

Gronroos, C. (1990), Relationship approach to marketing in service contexts: the marketing and organisation behavior interface. *Journal of Business Research*, **20**, 3–12.

Lawler, E. E., III. (1992), *The Ultimate Advantage: Creating the High Involvement Organisation*. The Jossey-Bass Management Series. San Francisco.

Maher, D. (1991), Service guarantees: double-barreled Standards. *Training*, **28**(6) 27–30.

Parasuraman, A., Berry, L. L. and Zeithaml, V. (1991), Understanding, measuring, improving service quality findings from a multiphase research program. In S. Brown, E. Gummesson, B. Edvardsson and B. Gustavsson (eds), *Service Quality: Multidisciplinary and Multinational Perspectives*. New York: Lexington Books.

Parasuraman, A., Zeithaml, V. A. and Berry, L. L. (1985). A conceptual model of service quality and its implications for future research. *Journal of Marketing*, **49**, Fall, 41–50.

Peters, T. (1989), *Thriving on Chaos*. New York: Pan Books.

Prahalad, C. K. and Hamel, G. (1990), The core competence of the corporation. *Harvard Business Review*, May–June, 79–91.

Solomon, M. R., Surprenanat, C., Czepiel, J. A. and Gutman, E. G. (1985), A role theory perspective on dynamic interactions: the service encounter. *Journal of Marketing*, **49**, 99–111.

World Tourism Organisation (1991), *Tourism to the year 2000: qualitative aspects affecting global growth*. Discussion paper.

Wren, J. (1988), Service-driven: management must gear to it. *Management*, October. New Zealand.

Zeithaml, V. A. and Bitner, M. J. (1996), *Services Marketing*. New York: McGraw-Hill.

Zeithaml, V. A., Berry, L. L. and Parasuraman, A. (1996), The behavioral consequences of service quality. *Journal of Marketing*, **60**, April, 31–46.

Zemke, R. and Schaaf, D. (1989), *The Service Edge: 101 Companies that Profit from Customer Care*. New York: Nal Books.

CHAPTER FOUR

Employing Graduates in Hospitality Small to Medium-sized Enterprises: Context and Issues

Rick Holden and Stephanie Jameson

INTRODUCTION

This chapter seeks to identify a number of critical issues in the employment and utilization of graduates in hospitality small to medium-sized enterprises (SMEs). To do this it is important to locate the theme in the wider context of the graduate labour market as a whole. The chapter is divided into two sections. The first section provides an overview of current issues pertinent to the graduate labour market in the UK. Mass higher education has brought new issues to the fore and intensified tensions that have existed for many years. Employment opportunities within SMEs are very much a topic of the time. In the second section of the chapter we look specifically at hospitality management graduates. As with the graduate labour market generally, the flow of more graduates into hospitality SMEs is topical, yet our understanding of this process is limited by lack of research. We raise a number of issues and questions about this process and in relation to prevailing assumptions that the future for graduate labour within hospitality will be dominated by small firms.

A changing graduate labour market

Higher education is playing an increasing role in providing knowledge and skills for entrants to the labour market. The UK now has a system of mass higher education with one in three young people entering university. Graduate numbers have increased in all subject areas, the most rapid growth taking place in business and business-related studies. Overall, graduate entrants to the labour market doubled between 1979 and 1996 (DfEE, 1998). Such growth has placed increasing pressure on the relationship between higher education and employers in terms of graduate employment. The questions 'Are there sufficient graduate jobs?' and 'Are the graduates adequately equipped for the jobs which they are offered?' are frequently asked. However, such questions are not new. The relationship between the supply of graduate labour and the demand for it has been a source of debate and some tension for many years. The central issue is one of matching: matching the skills, abilities and expectations of the graduate with the demands, requirements and expectations of the first destination employer. Research suggests this process is characteristically a source of expectation mismatch, ambiguity and tension (Arnold and MacKenzie Davey, 1992; Connor and Pollard, 1996). Employers report a skills gap: a mismatch between what they want of new graduates and their satisfaction with the levels shown by those they recruit. According to the independently produced *Graduate Employment and Training Report* (1998) employers find it difficult to recruit suitable numbers of graduates who can communicate in teams, analyse problems, or manage their learning of new skills. The Industrial Relations Services (1997a) report that their annual survey of graduate recruitment has consistently shown graduates' level of business awareness attracting most criticism from employers.

Whilst the rise in graduate numbers is a highly visible trend impacting upon this process, other significant changes have also been taking place in the graduate labour market. The graduate labour market is becoming increasingly fragmented, heterogeneous and complex. The key changes are summarized below:

- there are a greater number and more diverse range of graduates. New graduates are much more varied in terms of their background, age, methods of study, prior qualifications and ethnicity. Women, for example, now make up approximately 50 per cent of all graduates, compared with under 25 per cent ten years ago (Industrial Relations Services, 1996);
- fewer new graduates are securing traditional 'graduate' jobs: jobs for life with a large employer and a clear career path in a single function. Recent economic and structural changes have resulted in a reduction in recruitment by many of these employers (Williams and Owen, 1997). One important trend is for increasing numbers of graduates to find employment in SMEs. Small to medium-sized enterprises have become an important part of the UK economy and are now creating new jobs much faster than larger firms;

- methods of recruitment are changing. Contacts with education institutions are still commonly used but the traditional 'milkround' (where large recruiters undertake an extensive range of visits to UK colleges and universities, specifically to target their quota of graduates) has become increasingly less important. Employers are using more and more diverse sets of recruitment practices including specialist journals and the internet;
- many undergraduates now benefit from strong integration of transferable skills within their degree programmes in preparation for subsequent employment. Established in 1988, in part as a response to criticism of graduates levelled by employers, the government-funded Enterprise in Higher Education (EHE) programme has sought to enable students in higher education (whatever the discipline) to become lifelong learners and be better prepared for working life. Independent evaluation suggests EHE[1] has changed and is continuing to change curriculum, teaching methods and assessment (Whiteley, 1995).

The Dearing report in 1997 further reinforces the significance of such changes and highlights the overriding imperative for higher education in the UK to meet the needs of the society it serves (Industrial Relations Services, 1997b).

Utilization of graduate labour

Somewhat paradoxically we have a situation where on the one hand employers are complaining that graduates lack certain transferable skills, whilst on the other there is growing evidence of graduate under-employment and under-utilization. Research conducted by the National Institute of Economic and Social Research (Mason, 1996) deems graduates to be under-utilized if:

- they are employed in jobs for which university degrees have not usually been required;
- the jobs have not been substantially modified to take advantage of their skills and knowledge;
- no salary premium is offered compared with non-graduates in the same jobs.

They report considerable evidence of under-utilization of graduates in the financial services (and they argue, by implication, in the service industry generally). In banks and building societies, for example, up to 45 per cent of all graduates recruited were deemed to be working in unmodified clerical jobs. Broadly similar findings are presented by Dolton and Vignoles (1997) who note that executive officers in the civil service used to need only A levels whereas today they usually require a degree even though in many instances the actual job has changed very little.

An inevitable outcome of any system of mass higher education may be a proportion of 'over-educated' graduates. However, despite these and other similar findings, it is premature to claim we are producing too many graduates in the UK. Firstly, it is difficult to define what is and is not a 'graduate job' since much of the existing research relies on subjective self-surveys. Secondly, it is possible that graduates transform 'non-graduate' jobs over time because of the extra skills and knowledge they bring to the job. This is potentially of enormous significance where small firms recruit graduates to help them 'grow the business'.

SMEs and graduates

Overall, graduates are still under-represented within SMEs compared to larger firms or the public sector. An estimate by Williams and Owen (1997) puts the number of graduates working within SMEs at 8 per cent of the SME workforce compared with 13 per cent elsewhere. However, SMEs are increasingly an important part of the UK economy and are responsible for most of the growth in private sector employment (McLarty, 1997). Furthermore, small business sector employment is forecast to continue to grow at a healthy rate (Avery, 1994). There is a prevailing expectation, therefore, that SMEs will increasingly be a growth area for graduate employment.

One reason for the under-representation of graduates within SMEs is the generally negative perception of what a graduate can do and can offer the business. Graduates are perceived by many SME employers as:

- impractical;
- reluctant to get their hands dirty;
- slow to become productive;
- holding a poor view of what employment in an SME would be like.

It is not surprising that the degree of ambiguity and ambivalence with respect to feelings about graduates is more acute with SME employers. This is because they do not traditionally recruit graduates and often the employer or manager him/herself is not educated to degree level. Specific studies suggest that the problem may lie in the employers' perception of graduate capability in the 'softer' skills rather than any 'technical' deficiency. For example, a study of SMEs (Rajan, Chapple and Battersby, 1998) in London suggested that nearly 80 per cent felt graduates lacked motivation and

Table 4.1 SMEs' views on graduates

SMEs recruiting graduates	SMEs not recruiting graduates
• Graduates are intelligent and learn and adapt quickly	• The work done is unsuitable for graduates
• Graduates possess more technical skills	• Graduates lack work experience
• Graduates sometimes expect too high a salary	• Graduates are unrealistic about salary levels
• Graduates bring ideas and imagination	• Graduates might bring new ideas, specialist skills and high level learning
• Graduates have good communication skills	• Graduates would become quickly disillusioned and leave

Source: DfEE (1998)

drive. Almost 90 per cent of the SMEs polled cited the graduates' communication skills as needing the most enhancement, whilst 83 per cent and 85 per cent respectively considered that graduates lacked teamwork and self-management skills.

The DfEE's (1998) research on the recruitment and utilization of graduates in SMEs points out that firms who have recruited graduates hold somewhat different views from those who have not. These views are summarized in Table 4.1. Both agree, however, that students and graduates need to be proactive in approaching SMEs and more realistic about salary expectations. Only 9 per cent of respondents expressed an active preference for not recruiting a graduate. This suggests that there is scope for raising awareness amongst employers of the benefits graduates could bring to their businesses. This theme is discussed at the end of this section.

Typically, SMEs are reliant on informal and unsystematic recruitment methods (Curran, Kitching, Abbot and Mills, 1993; Lucas, 1995). Sophisticated mechanisms and processes often characterize the large firm's recruitment of graduates and can be carried out by a specialist. In contrast, graduates are recruited into SMEs using *ad hoc* and unstructured processes. Such difficulties may be compounded by non-existent or poorly developed training and development systems. We have already noted that SMEs may well expect any newly recruited graduate to make an immediate contribution to the business. However, SMEs generally have no formal induction programmes or structured training and development programme for the graduate to follow.

Although based on research with large employers, the significance of the role of the line manager in effectively inducting the graduate into his or her new position is evident. Preston (1994) suggests the line manger should be regarded as the 'pivotal' element in organizational socialization, whilst Graham and McKenzie (1995) note that however sophisticated the formal framework of graduate development provision, the role of the graduate's direct manager is of critical importance in ensuring a successful transition. Within an SME it is suggested such a role may be even more significant. For example, Gold, Whitehouse and Hill (1996) note that the relationship between the graduate and the managing director may be the *locus* of 'distortions' that hamper success.

Small to medium-sized enterprises are expected to absorb an increasingly larger share of the annual graduate output. Therefore, there is an emerging consensus that stronger links between SMEs and higher education will encourage higher levels of graduate recruitment and ensure a closer match of expectations between the graduate and the employer.

Enhancing the graduate labour market

Change is now regarded as a characteristic of most organizational life. Wherever graduates work, they must be equipped to respond to and manage such change. Partly based on responses from employers, but also on its own assessment of how they see the nature of work changing as we approach the millennium, the Association of Graduate Recruiters (AGR) has compiled a profile of what it considers the skills required by the graduate in the twenty-first century. The association considers that 'self reliance' skills are the enabling skills which will be essential for graduates to survive in the twenty-first century. In the context of this chapter it is important to note that the AGR suggest such skills are equally, if not more, important with respect to graduate employment in SMEs. A summary of these skills is shown in Table 4.2.

Table 4.2 Self reliance skills

• Self-awareness	• Self-promotion
• Exploring and creating opportunities	• Action planning
• Networking	• Matching and decision-making
• Negotiating	• Political awareness
• Coping with uncertainty	• Focus of development
• Transfer skills	• Self-confidence

Source: DfEE (1996)

The second half of the 1990s has seen a plethora of initiatives aimed specifically at the SME in relation to graduate employment. Key objectives in all such initiatives are to address the barriers to the recruitment of graduates by SMEs; establish a better understanding between SMEs and higher education; and thereby stimulate demand for graduate labour. Examples of such initiatives include:

- *Using Graduate Skills:* a project (1996–98) aimed at enhancing employment levels and employability of graduates in SMEs by establishing an effective national network of committed and informed Training and Education Council (TEC) staff who could influence TEC and Business Link strategies in relation to the SME graduate labour market;
- *Graduate Link:* established in 1996 and seeking to help companies invest in the future by recruiting graduates. It acts on behalf of all the universities and colleges in Yorkshire, offering managed access to a vast pool of graduates;
- *Teaching Company Scheme:* a government-funded programme which enables a graduate to join an SME for two years to work on a development which is strategically important to the company but which demands additional knowledge and skilled labour. Many other initiatives run by individual TECs or universities similarly seek to place graduates with SMEs for fixed periods or organize placements with SMEs.

HOSPITALITY MANAGEMENT EDUCATION

Demand and supply

In a report commissioned by the hospitality industry, the Higher Education Funding Council (HEFC) (1998) estimate that the UK hospitality industry needs to fill something like 34,000 managerial posts a year. However, they estimate that 'output' from college-based courses is likely to meet under 7 per cent of the demand for qualified managers. Using the Higher Education Statistics Agency subject category N7 (Catering and Institutional Management), Littlejohn and Morrison (1997) report 16,445 undergraduates and 948 postgraduates studying in the UK for academic year 1995–96. This category, however, covers much more than hospitality management. More useful as an indication of the extent to which higher education is attempting to meet the demand for managers is the census of hospitality undergraduates, also undertaken by Littlejohn and Morrison. Albeit based only on students registered in England, the authors identified 8356 students enrolled on 79 courses in 27 higher and further education institutions in England. Of these, 5626 students were studying at degree level and 2730 were following diploma courses. On the basis of a four-year degree programme and a three-year diploma programme, this implies an annual output of 2000–3000 graduates and diplomats in the subject. In practice the number is somewhat lower as only approximately two-thirds go directly into employment (Belfield, 1997). Cooper, Njau and Rowlty (1998) support these numbers and estimate an additional 60–5 per cent of graduates move directly into the industry upon graduation.

The degree programme

Graduates enter the labour market from an enormous range of degree disciplines. One estimate puts the number of graduates who gain employment with non-specific or generalist degrees as high as 50 per cent. Elsewhere, there is a closer link between industry and degree discipline, and this is the case with hospitality management. Brennan and McGeevor (1987) present four broad categories in which the employment status of graduates may be placed. These are generalist, generalist plus, occupational generalist and occupational specialist. Table 4.3 (p. 56) presents these four categories. Each category relates to the skills and knowledge that the graduate has acquired during his/her degree education. This has subsequent value to the graduate in seeking and obtaining a job in the labour market. Hospitality degree courses can be located in the occupational generalist category. Hospitality undergraduates illustrate a commitment to the hotel and catering industry in their choice of degree. Although at this stage they might not have a precise occupational role in mind, they have demonstrated a clear commitment to a specific field of employment.

An important feature of the occupational generalist category in Brennan and McGeevor's model is that graduates will have acquired skills and knowledge specific to the industry during their degree programme. Three key features of hospitality management degree/diploma programmes are summarized below:

- *generic underpinning:* most departments provide a first year which is generic to hospitality, allowing specialization in industry sectors in subsequent years;
- *practical training:* differentiates hospitality management from mainstream business and management courses and is central to the culture of a

hospitality management school. Littlejohn and Morrison (1997) report that, on average, 23 per cent of student contact hours are 'laboratory' based (i.e. learning set firmly in the kitchen, restaurant, bar, accommodation and reception settings). Increasingly, departments provide specialist information technology training, including electronic point of sale, customer flow analysis, and computer-assisted design for facilities management;

- *supervised work experience:* placement opportunities enable students to integrate theory and practice and develop important transferable skills (e.g. interpersonal skills, problem solving). Littlejohn and Morrison (1997) estimate that 75 per cent of courses require students to spend 46–50 weeks in industry, with a further 18 per cent requiring 36–45 weeks.

Table 4.3 Four graduate employment categories

Generalist	*Generalist plus*
• Equipped with general skills of value to employment but not especially related to any employment field • Process of seeking, obtaining and becoming competent in a job only begins upon graduation	• Graduates also have certain specialist skills applicable to work • Element of occupational training in this type of degree course and the prospect of a closer tie-up between course content and job requirement • Process of seeking, obtaining and becoming competent in a job begins at graduation
Occupational generalist	*Occupational specialist*
• First step towards a particular job with graduate's choice of degree course • Imprecise ideas relating to a general employment field rather than a precise, occupational role • After graduation, continuing choices about further specialization • Graduate has demonstrated commitment to a broad field of employment and has knowledge and skills of specialist value to work	• Graduates received partial job training and their degree qualification regulates entry into the job • Choice of career occurs at entry point to higher education • After graduation there are likely to be clearly defined steps to acquire full professional status and a job

Adapted from: Brennan and McGeevor (1987)

It should also be noted that in recent years (and prompted in large part by the Enterprise in Higher Education programme) considerable innovation has been introduced into hospitality management education programmes. For example, Brotherton (1995) reports a number of case studies where objectives have been to promote experiential learning and transferable skills and which focus attention on the importance of appropriate partnerships with hospitality companies as means to facilitate such ends.

However, despite these features and characteristics of hospitality management education, hospitality graduates have not been immune to the more widespread criticisms levelled at graduates and noted in the previous section. Jameson (1996) notes the existence of a 'recurrent debate' surrounding the degree of 'fit' between hospitality graduates and the perceptions of hospitality employers. Basically, there is a perceived mismatch between the skills, knowledge and attitudes which the hospitality graduate has to offer, and the skills, knowledge and attitudes which the industry thinks it needs. However, the significance of the large employer in this debate must be noted as potentially distorting our view of the labour market. As with graduates generally, it is inappropriate to treat the hospitality industry as a homogeneous group of organizations and hospitality graduates as a homogenous mass of individuals.

Graduate employment in hospitality SMEs

From Purcell and Quinn's (1995) research it is known that hospitality graduates are employed in small firms. At the time of their survey it was estimated that 31 per cent of hospitality graduates worked in organizations with fewer than 100 employees, and a total of 50 per cent of hospitality graduates worked in the SME sector. Even though the industry is dominated by small independent operators, research in the hospitality industry has been located in the context of large multinational enterprises (Jameson, 1996). The propensity to use large firms as the research base mirrors studies of the transition and utilization of graduates more generally. Lack of research in SMEs is unfortunate because this sector is expected to employ increasing numbers of graduates. Nevertheless, there is sufficient insight to identify a number of key issues and questions which are discussed below.

What is taught

Jameson (1996) and Peacock (1996) argue that the influence of large multinational enterprises within industry is reflected in the teaching and learning strategies of hospitality educators. Supporting evidence is provided by findings from our own research (Holden and Jameson, 1998) which sought to address the transition of graduates from hospitality education into employment within hospitality SMEs. Hospitality graduates were questioned about their undergraduate courses and the relevance they were perceived to have for managing SMEs. Interestingly, the graduates rated prior, pre-degree education as more important than their degree programme. For example one graduate commented:

> Mine was all 'take your company to Europe blah blah blah ...' like for heads of massive companies. It was very interesting, but nothing I could use. The HND [Higher National Diploma] is what I am using now. I am not using my degree and I don't suppose I ever will. My degree was a very good degree but it's very strategic and it's very forward looking ... it wasn't hands on day to day.

When asked about their degree and the extent to which small firms had been included in the programme, the influence of the large firm was again apparent:

> Basically, looking at things like financial management and human resource management it's all multinationals. That's all it is. Thinking about it, you don't do anything that relates to small businesses. Everything was aimed at your big chains like Trusthouse Forte.

> ... I think a lot though was that any information you needed off CD–ROM or anything you could only get information on large companies anyway, so you had to work, you had to stick to them, if you wanted to make doing your assignment as easy as possible.

Graduates also commented about representatives of companies, who were also predominantly from large enterprises, coming to speak to them in their final year.

Supervised work experience and SMEs

Purcell and Quinn (1995) examined supervised work experience, linking organizational size and qualifications. They discovered that students on degree courses were more likely to spend all or part of their experience in large hotels. On the other hand, students undertaking Higher National Diplomas (HNDs) tended to work in small hotels. The significance of the placement goes beyond the development of certain core and transferable skills. For example, West and Jameson (1990) discovered that students' experiences determined their decision to pursue a career in hospitality management. Purcell and Quinn (1995) found that 'good' placement experience is likely to result in students remaining in this sector after graduation. According to their study, when placement experience is examined against subsequent retention and employment in the industry, there is a clear indication that small hotels have a high retention rate. These authors suggest that student choice of placement is crucial to employers and industrial tutors. In other words, more students need to be positioned within hospitality SMEs for their periods of industrial placement.

Utilization of graduates in hospitality SMEs

Thus far we have not sought to question the prevailing assumption that more and more graduates will find employment in SMEs. However, the findings from our research on the transition of graduates into hospitality SMEs cast some doubt on the legitimacy and appropriateness of such assumptions. Although confirming that systematic human resource (HR) practices are more likely than not to be absent in SMEs, our findings sit less comfortably with existing research on the transition of graduates into employment, with the presumed difficulties faced by graduates in the SME labour market, and with strongly held beliefs that hospitality management degrees equip students for jobs in hospitality management. Despite a lack of formal HR processes and procedures, our graduates were performing well in both their eyes and those of their managers. Notwithstanding prevailing assumptions that SMEs do not understand graduates and that graduates do not understand SMEs, the situation in these case studies suggested such claims, even if true, impact minimally on transition and performance.

The key issue is one of utilization. It is our contention that these graduates were under-utilized: that their job context was simply less demanding and stretching than might have been expected for a graduate working within an SME, with considerable amounts of time being spent on routine, repetitive work. We question, therefore, the extent to which hospitality SMEs may be capable of utilizing graduate labour appropriately. Earlier in this chapter, evidence of graduate under-employment and under-utilization was noted. In a study of graduate labour Connor and Pollard (1996) report that the highest level of 'under-employment' is in the sector of distribution, hotels and catering where 80 per cent felt 'under-employed'.

Based on our research, three possible scenarios for graduate employment in the hospitality SME sector may be identified. The first is where a graduate works in a stable small firm. These firms dominate the hospitality industry and the small firms sector in a number of other industries. In these cases we found graduates relying heavily on pre-degree learning and using a range of low-level technical, rather than managerial, skills. We speculate that within this type of organization graduates are, and are likely to remain, under-utilized. Imaginative practices such as SME networks are needed to avoid high levels of new graduate entrant turnover. The second scenario is that of graduates employed in SMEs which have 'growth potential'. In this case, graduates may bring new knowledge, skills and ideas into the business, help nurture its growth and thus add value to the firm. In a small number of cases these prospects were evident but we know little about the dynamics of the process. However, this situation highlights a critical factor which is central to the following scenario where a small firm has an explicit strategy to grow and is currently enjoying a period of growth. Although growth firms form the minority amongst SMEs, they offer graduates the greatest potential for application of their skills and future personal development. Growth firms are also those offering the greatest potential for job creation in the future. However, our study identified under-utilized graduates in this sector. In our research, graduates performed 'comfortably' but were nonetheless under-utilized. The transition and utilization of graduates within hospitality SMEs remain problematic even in growth firms.

SUMMARY

Any attempt to understand current trends and issues pertinent to the transition of hospitality graduates into employment in SMEs needs to begin from an understanding of the graduate labour market more generally. Graduates now face a less predictable, more rapidly changing and more competitive labour market than did their predecessors even a decade ago. Mass higher education and a host of other changes in terms of who is a graduate and what they study while at university have combined to make this a market in transition. The fact that within the hospitality industry increasing numbers of hospitality graduates are being employed by SMEs is not in doubt. There is a prevailing assumption that this trend will continue. However, this particular segment of the graduate labour market reflects many of the tensions and uncertainties seen more widely. Whilst the basic structures of hospitality management programmes provide a sound basis for subsequent employment in hospitality SMEs, these organizations, the problems they face, and the beneficial value of the work placement require in future more attention on degree programmes. If hospitality SMEs are to fully utilize graduate labour, further efforts are necessary on the supply and demand side of the labour market. Employers' misgivings about the value of recruiting graduates must be addressed by the provision of supervised work experience and by establishing stronger links with educators. However, SMEs using graduates to undertake non-graduate jobs may have to adjust their working practices so that individuals can 'grow' on the job. Otherwise graduates will be lost to other companies offering superior training, development and progression opportunities.

Note

1 EHE, a government-funded initiative, formally concluded in 1996. However, its legacy continues in many institutions of higher education.

REFERENCES

Arnold, J. and Mackenzie Davey, K. (1992), Beyond unmet expectations: a detailed analysis of graduate experiences during the first three years of their careers. *Personnel Review*, **21**(2), 45–68.

Avery, L. (1994), *Small Firms Survey: Employment – The View of the Small Firm*. British Chambers of Commerce.

Belfield, C. (1997), Employment in small and medium sized enterprises – what do graduates think? *Higher Education and Employment Network News*, 1 July.

Brennan, J. and McGeevor, P. A. (1987), *CNAA Graduates: Their Employment and Their Experience After Leaving College*. Summary Report, Publication No. 13, CNAA.

Brotherton, B. (1995), Hospitality management education. *Education and Training*, **37**(4), 4–5.

Connor, H. and Pollard, E. (1996), *What Do Graduates Really Do?*, Report Number 308, Institute of Employment Studies, Brighton.

Cooper, D., Njau, M. and Rowley, G. (1998), Analysis of HESA counts and first employment destinations for hospitality management students, Working paper, Higher Education Funding Council, Bristol.

Curran, J., Kitching, J., Abbot, B. and Mills, V. (1993), *Employment and*

Employment Relations in the Small Service Sector Enterprise – A Report. ESRC Centre for Research on Small Service Sector Enterprises, Kingston.

Department for Education and Employment (DfEE) (1996), Skills for graduates in the 21st century. *Skills and Enterprise Briefing*, Issue 31.

Department for Education and Employment (DfEE) (1998), *Labour Market and Skill Trends*, 1997/98. DfEE, Sheffield.

Dolton, P. and Vignoles, A. (1997), *Over-education: Problem or Not?* Society for Research into Higher Education.

Graduate Employment and Training Report: Towards the Millennium (1998), Hobson's Publishing.

Gold, J., Whitehouse, N. and Hill, B. (1996), If the CAPS fit . . .: learning to manage in SMEs. *Education & Training*, 38(9), 26–33.

Graham, C. and McKenzie, A. (1995), Delivering the promise: developing new graduates. *Education & Training*, 37(2), 33–40.

Higher Education Funding Council (HEFC) 1998, *Review of Hospitality Management*, April. HEFC, Bristol.

Holden, R. J. and Jameson, S. (1998), Questioning current assumptions on the transition of graduates into SME employment: the case of hospitality. *7th Annual Hospitality Research Conference Proceedings*. Glasgow Caledonian University.

Industrial Relations Services (1996), Graduate recruitment and sponsorship: the 1996 IRS survey on employer practice. *Employee Development Bulletin*, 83. London.

Industrial Relations Services (1997a), Graduate recruitment and sponsorship: the 1997 IRS survey on employer practice. *Employee Development Bulletin*, 95. London.

Industrial Relations Services (1997b), Goodbye to all that: higher education after Dearing. *Employee Development Bulletin*, 92. London.

Jameson, S. M. (1996), Small firms and the hospitality graduate labour market. Viewpoint, *International Journal of Contemporary Hospitality Management*, 8(5), 37–8.

Littlejohn, D. and Morrison, J. (1997), *Hospitality Management Education Report*. Council for Hospitality Management.

Lucas, R. (1995), *Managing Employee Relations in the Hotel and Catering Industry*. London: Cassell.

Mason, G. (1996), *Graduate Utilisation in British industry: The Critical Impact of Mass Higher Education*, May. National Institute Economic Review, NIESR, London.

McLarty, R. (1997), The Suffolk working smarter project. *Higher Education and Employment Network News*, 1 July.

Peacock, J. (1996), In defence of the hospitality business independent: a personal view. *International Journal of Hospitality Management*, **8**(2), 31–6.

Preston, A. (1994), Learning the organisation: confusions and contradictions for new managers. *Human Resource Management Journal*, **4**(1), 24–33.

Purcell, K. and Quinn, J. (1995), *Hospitality Management and Employment Trajectories*. Oxford: Oxford Brookes University.

Rajan, A., Chapple, K. and Battersby, I. (1998), *Graduates in Growing Companies: The Rhetoric of Core Skills and Reality of Globalisation*. Centre for Research in Employment and Technology in Europe, London.

West, A. and Jameson, S. M. (1990), Supervised work experience in graduate employment. *International Journal of Contemporary Hospitality Management*, **2**(2), 29–32.

Williams, H. and Owen, G. (1997), *Recruitment and Utilisation of Graduates by Small and Medium Sized Enterprises*. Research Report No. 29, DfEE.

Whiteley, T. (1995), Enterprise in higher education – an overview from the Department for Education and Employment. *Education & Training*, **37**(9), 4–8.

PART TWO
Strategy

CHAPTER FIVE

Motivation:
Theory and Practice

Julia Christensen Hughes

Motivated 'having a definite and positive desire to do things'. (Oxford American Dictionary, 1980, p. 434)

Motivation 'a person's desire to accomplish a task or achieve a goal. Motivation energizes, directs and sustains human behaviour'. (Gomez-Mejia, Balkin, Cardy and Dimick, 1997, p. 27)

Motivate '1. to give a motive or incentive to, to be the motive of. 2. to stimulate the interest of, to inspire'. (Oxford American Dictionary, 1980, p. 434)

INTRODUCTION

Motivation is at the root of conscious human behaviour. As such, in order to become truly self-aware, people must understand their own motivations. For people who wish to become effective managers, it is also important to understand the motivations of others.

Motivated employees are an essential attribute of any successful organization. Management's job is to create the context within which employees will strive to contribute to the goals of the organization. In other words, by influencing the context, and hiring the right employees, managers can affect the degree to which employees feel motivated to 'do the best possible job or to exert the maximum effort to perform assigned tasks' (Gomez-Mejia *et al.*, 1997, p. 88). Perhaps nowhere is understanding employee motivation more important than in customer service oriented businesses, such as the hospitality industry, where front-line employees have an immediate impact on customer satisfaction. Hospitality managers need to be skilled at creating contexts in which their employees feel constantly motivated to provide superior levels of customer service and product quality. Contributing to this challenge is the diverse nature of employees in the hospitality industry: what motivates one person does not necessarily motivate another. Gender, age, part-time versus full-time status, and cultural background are some of the personal attributes that can significantly influence motivation. This chapter begins with a discussion of the impact of culture on motivation.

The impact of culture on motivation

Geert Hofstede (1984) has made an enormous contribution to our understanding of the impact that culture and values can have on motivation. In 1968, and again in 1972, Hofstede surveyed over 116,000 employees from 40 different countries. These employees worked in a variety of occupations (i.e. sales, service, administration, management – all levels) for the same multinational. In analysing the results, Hofstede identified four discrete dimensions of national culture: power distance, uncertainty avoidance, individualism and masculinity. Controlling for occupation, each country was assigned a score for these dimensions using either 'mean scores on five-point quasi-interval scales or percentages of answers on nominal scales' (Hofstede, 1984, p. 54). The relative position of each country vis-à-vis these dimensions can help us better understand the profound effect of culture on motivation.

Power distance

Hofstede's power distance dimension deals with inequality. Employees from high power distance cultures are comfortable with inequality (i.e. they prefer centralized power structures, hierarchies, status symbols, and privileges for the few), while employees from low power distance cultures prefer decentralized power structures, 'flat' organizations, and equal privileges. Table 5.1 shows how this cultural dimension is reflected in the workplace. Employees from low power distance countries are motivated by the opportunity to give input. Employees from high power distance countries are assumed not to be motivated, hence the need for close supervision. With a mean score of 51, the countries that ranked highest on power distance include the Philippines (94), Mexico (81), Venezuela (81), India (77) and Singapore (74). Countries that ranked lowest include Ireland (28), New Zealand (22), Denmark (18), Israel (13) and Austria (11). Moderate to low scores were received by the USA (40), Canada (39), Australia (36) and Great Britain (35).

Table 5.1 Motivation dimension: power distance

Low power distance countries	High power distance countries
• Managers make decisions after consulting with subordinates	• Managers make decisions autocratically and paternalistically
• Close supervision negatively evaluated by subordinates	• Close supervision positively evaluated by subordinates
• Stronger perceived work ethic; strong disbelief that people dislike work	• Weaker perceived work ethic; frequent belief that people dislike work
• Employees less afraid of disagreeing with their boss	• Employees fear disagreeing with their boss
• Employees show more co-operativeness	• Employees reluctant to trust each other

Uncertainty avoidance

Hofstede's uncertainty avoidance dimension targets comfort with uncertainty. Employees from high uncertainty avoidance cultures are uncomfortable with uncertainty (i.e. they value rules, law, order, security, absolute truths, and expertise) while employees from low uncertainty avoidance cultures value as few rules as possible, relativism, and common sense. Table 5.2 (p. 70) shows how these values are reflected in the workplace. Employees from countries with low uncertainty avoidance are motivated by the need for achievement, and by opportunities for advancement. When their needs are not met, they are quick to leave for opportunities elsewhere. Employees from countries with high uncertainty avoidance are motivated by loyalty and rules. With a mean score of 64, the countries that ranked highest on uncertainty avoidance include Greece (112), Portugal (104), Belgium (94), Japan (92) and Peru (87). Countries that ranked lowest include Great Britain (35), Ireland (35), Hong Kong (29), Sweden (29), Denmark (23) and Singapore (8). Moderate to low scores were received by Australia (51), New Zealand (49), Canada (48) and the USA (46).

Individualism

According to Hofstede individualism 'describes the relationship between the individual and the collectivity which prevails in a given society' (1984, p. 148). Employees from high individualism cultures value the rights and needs of the individual. Employees from low individualism cultures value

Table 5.2 Motivation dimension: uncertainty avoidance

Low uncertainty avoidance countries	*High uncertainty avoidance countries*
• Lower job stress	• Higher job stress
• Less emotional resistance to change	• More emotional resistance to change
• Less hesitation to change employers	• Tendency to stay with same employer
• Loyalty to employer is not seen as a virtue	• Loyalty to employer is seen as a virtue
• Preference for smaller organizations as employers	• Preference for larger organizations
• Lower average age in higher level jobs	• Higher average age in higher level jobs
• Stronger achievement motivation	• Less achievement motivation
• Stronger ambition for individual advancement	• Lower ambition for individual advancement
• Rules may be broken for pragmatic reasons	• Company rules should not be broken

Table 5.3 Motivation dimension: individualism

Low individualism	*High individualism*
• Importance of provisions by company (training, physical conditions)	• Importance of employees' personal time
• Emotional dependence on company	• Emotional independence from company
• Large company attractive	• Small company attractive
• More importance attached to training and skills	• More importance attached to freedom and challenge
• Managers do not support employee initiative	• Managers stimulate employee initiative
• Individual initiative is socially frowned upon	• Individual initiative is socially encouraged

the rights and needs of the group. Table 5.3 shows how this is reflected in the workplace. Employees from low individualism countries are motivated by the opportunity to learn new skills and to contribute to the needs of the group. Employees from high individualism countries are motivated by personal needs, challenge, and the opportunity to exercise initiative. With a mean score of 54, the countries that ranked highest on individualism include the USA (91), Australia (90), Great Britain (89), Canada (80) and the

Table 5.4 Motivation dimension: masculinity

Low masculinity	High masculinity
• Relationship with manager, co-operation, friendly atmosphere, living in a desirable area, and employment security relatively more important	• Earnings, recognition, advancement, and challenge relatively more important
• Weaker achievement motivation	• Stronger achievement motivation
• Achievement defined in terms of human contacts and living environment	• Achievement defined in terms of recognition and wealth
• Work less central in people's lives	• Greater work centrality in people's lives
• People prefer shorter working hours to more salary	• People prefer more salary to shorter working hours
• Like small companies	• Like large corporations
• Lower job stress	• Higher job stress
• Smaller or no value differences between men and women in the same job	• Greater value differences between men and women in the same job

Netherlands (80). Countries that ranked lowest include Taiwan (17), Peru (16), Pakistan (14), Colombia (13) and Venezuela (12). Moderate scores were received by Austria (55), Israel (54), Spain (51), India (48) and Japan (46).

Masculinity

Lastly, the masculinity dimension is concerned with the extent to which 'respondents in a country (of both sexes) tend to endorse goals usually more popular among men [high masculinity] or among women [low masculinity]' (Hofstede, 1984, p. 176). Employees from high masculinity cultures value money and things, performance and growth, achievement and independence. Employees from low masculinity cultures value people, quality of life, the environment, service and interdependence. Table 5.4 shows how this is reflected in the workplace. Employees from countries with low masculinity scores are motivated by relationships, quality of life, and activities outside work. Employees from countries with high masculinity scores are motivated by wealth, recognition, and achievement. With a mean score of 51, the countries that ranked highest on masculinity include Japan (95), Austria (79), Venezuela (73), Italy (70) and Switzerland (70). Countries that ranked lowest include Finland (26), Denmark (16), Netherlands (14), Norway (8) and Sweden (5). Moderate to high scores were received by

Ireland (68), Great Britain (66), the USA (62), Australia (61), New Zealand (58) and Canada (52).

In summary, motivation is strongly influenced by culture. What employees from one national culture may find motivating may be demotivating to employees from another. Hofstede (1984, p. 256) emphasized this finding by drawing together the uncertainty avoidance and masculinity dimensions. Employees who are influenced by cultural values promoted in the USA and Great Britain, for example, are likely to be motivated by individual success in the form of wealth, recognition, and self-actualization. Employees from North European countries are likely to be motivated by the quality of their human relationships, the environment and a sense of belonging. It is also interesting to note that employee preference for smaller organizations was found to be related to the low masculinity, high individualism, and low uncertainty avoidance dimensions. Countries matching with at least two of these dimensions include Great Britain, Sweden, the Netherlands and Denmark. In reviewing the attributes of these dimensions, it appears that some people may prefer working for small companies in order to feel connected with others and to enjoy a higher quality of life (i.e. low masculinity). Others may prefer working for small companies in order to experience more freedom (i.e. high individualism), while others still may do so for opportunities for achievement and advancement (i.e. low uncertainty avoidance).

Managers of hospitality and tourism small to medium-sized enterprises (SMEs) would be well advised to reflect on these potentially conflicting values as they design motivational programmes. They should also acknowledge their own cultural values and biases. My own cultural background (I am a Canadian with British heritage) undoubtedly influences my perceptions of motivation, in terms of the theories I prefer and the assumptions I make about what employees will find motivational. One further important point about culture is that many of the best-known theories of motivation were written before the impact of culture was fully recognized. As a result, many are ethnocentric; they are presented as being universally applicable when in fact they are based on the experiences of employees from one particular country or cultural background – often the USA. Perhaps through growing internationalism (e.g. global trade, travel, and immigration), these differences will diminish over time. Cultures evolve and individuals' needs and values change. For now, the best we can do is to keep these limitations in mind as we review and attempt to apply theoretical concepts.

How does motivation occur?

To acquire a better understanding of motivation as a concept, consider the following question and possible responses: How motivated are you as a student?

- highly motivated?
- somewhat motivated?
- neither motivated nor demotivated?
- somewhat demotivated?
- highly demotivated?

In trying to answer this question you probably found yourself thinking that as a student you tend to have one level of motivation (one hopes 'highly' or 'somewhat' motivated), but in a particular course, with a particular instructor, at a particular time in the semester, or even on a particular day, your level of motivation may vary. Gomez-Mejia *et al.* (1997, p. 187) consider:

> If you are a typical student, your motivation to work hard in a class depends to a large extent on whether you like the course content, how much you like and respect your instructor, and the way in which grades are determined. Your academic ability is fairly stable from course to course, but your motivation level is much more variable.

If this description matches your experience, then you have already discovered that motivation is not a static phenomenon but a 'dynamic internal state' which results from a complex interaction between individual heredity-based factors and environmental factors. Kanfer (1992, p. 3) delineates these factors as well as the nature of their interaction:

> At the broadest level, an individual's motivation for a specific task or job is determined by environment, heredity, and their interactions (such as learning). These factors influence individual characteristics such as personality, motives, affect, attitudes, beliefs, knowledge, skills, and abilities. In turn, these characteristics affect one's choice of goals and actions, the intensity and character of effort, and the endurance of goal-directed behaviour over time.

Kanfer (1992) further sorts these factors into two groups: distal constructs and proximal constructs. Distal constructs have an indirect impact on behaviour and performance, and include the individual characteristics listed above as well as such factors as cultural background and values. Distal constructs interact directly with contextual factors (i.e. the nature of the task) and impact motivation through their influence on cognitive choices and intentions (e.g. work ethic). In other words, your intentions for achievement in a certain course can be explained, in large part, by the interaction between your heredity-based characteristics (e.g. a predisposition to work hard) and course-based factors (e.g. the enthusiasm of the instructor). Your intentions for achievement, in turn, are translated into specific goals (e.g. I want to achieve an A), and volition (e.g. I will stay in tonight to study). (Volition is defined as 'use of one's own will in choosing or making a decision' (Oxford American Dictionary, 1980, p. 777).) These latter factors (goal setting and volition) are known as proximal constructs because they have a direct impact on behaviour.

The link between proximal constructs and actual task performance is a topic of increasing interest to researchers. While many questions remain to be explored, what is known is that the link between volition and performance is mediated by situational constraints or contextual factors. For example, you may have the requisite ability and be willing to work hard, but any one of a number of factors (e.g. a bad cold, a deleted computer file, an argument with a friend, a misinterpretation of the assignment) may prevent you from 'performing' at your full potential. This situation can be expressed as follows:

$$\text{Performance} = f\ (\text{motivation} \times \text{ability} \times \text{situational constraints})$$

In the next section, specific theories of motivation are reviewed.

MOTIVATION THEORIES

Although there has been much interest in motivation theory over the past 40 years or so in management and industrial psychology literatures, no individual theory adequately captures the full complexity suggested in the preceding discussion. Rather, as Locke and Henne (1986) claim, because of this over-simplification, theorists have typically chosen to focus on a limited number of factors in this complex interplay. Motivation literature contains a vast array of theories that can be overlapping, disjointed, and contradictory. Regardless, motivation theories can provide helpful 'spring-boards' for self-reflection. They can also help identify potential catalysts and barriers to motivation in the workplace.

In this section several theories of motivation will be reviewed. Rather than an exhaustive treatment, only select theories will be presented. For more extensive discussions see Campbell and Pritchard (1976), Hackman and Oldham (1976), Deci and Ryan (1980), Locke, Shaw, Saari and Latham

(1981), and Landy and Becker (1990). The framework for the discussion will follow Kanfer's (1992) framework of distal and proximal constructs.

Distal constructs

Some of the earliest theories of motivation sought to link motivation to the interaction of personality-based factors and environmental concerns. Kanfer's (1992) framework divides personality-based motivation theories into three types: *dispositional*, *motive* and *choice* theories.

Dispositional theories

Dispositional theories are concerned with the interaction between 'natural tendencies' or 'inclinations' and environmental factors. One of the best known dispositional theories is Maslow's hierarchy of needs.

Abraham Maslow (1954) proposed five basic needs which can be arranged in a hierarchy. The most basic needs are physiological (e.g. food, water, air, shelter); security (e.g. safety, stability, absence of threat); affiliation (e.g. friendship, love, a sense of belonging); esteem (e.g. feelings of achievement and self-worth); and finally, self-actualization (e.g. self-fulfilment). Maslow further suggested the existence of a satisfaction–progression process whereby a person must achieve satisfaction with one level of need before progressing to the next. Consider how Maslow's theory relates to your experiences as a student. A well-organized, enthusiastic teacher may not be able to motivate an able student to work hard on an assignment if the student has not had adequate sleep or food, is concerned for their personal safety, or is distracted by a conflict with a close friend or family member.

Clayton Alderfer's ERG (Existence/Relatedness/Growth) theory (1972) was a revision and simplification of Maslow's original model into just three levels: existence, such as material needs; relatedness, such as interpersonal needs; and growth opportunities for unique personal development. Alderfer further suggested that in addition to a satisfaction–progression process, frustration–regression was also possible. In other words, failure to attain need satisfaction at one level could result in increased attention being given to lower level needs.

Interestingly, most text books that deal with motivation include both Maslow's hierarchy of needs and Alderfer's ERG theory, despite the fact that empirical research has failed to confirm most of their respective propositions (Landy and Becker, 1990). Schaffer (1953) discovered that rather than five or three levels, worker satisfaction may be understood by

Table 5.5 Managerial initiatives

Need	Contextual factor
Physiological/Existence	Discounted employee meals Work schedules that provide adequate time for rest/sleep Health plans Adequate pay
Security/Existence	Atmosphere of trust Due process in all human resource decisions Regular performance evaluations and employee feedback Off-hours transportation assistance Harassment free workplace
Affiliation/Relatedness	Social events Collaborative/team environment Work schedules that provide adequate family time Language support (such as English as a Second Language lessons – so that employees can communicate with one another)
Esteem/Growth	Recognition (saying thank you, giving public praise) Valuing employee diversity
Self-Actualization/Growth	Designing jobs that match employees' unique talents and interests; providing challenging assignments

knowing his or her two most important needs and the extent to which these needs are being met. However, Maslow (1965) is not dogmatic about his theory and recognizes its limitations, conceding that variations probably exist. If Maslow is correct, several interesting ideas for motivating employees can be gleaned from these theories. For example, managers who attempt to understand their employees' needs, and create contexts in which these needs can be met, will be more likely to have motivated employees than those who do not. Based on this premise, and using the needs identified by Maslow and Alderfer as a starting point, managers might consider adopting some of the initiatives summarized in Table 5.5.

Much current research on dispositional theories is concerned with identifying a core set of basic personality dimensions and exploring these dimensions' links with motivation and job performance. In a manner similar to the earliest discussions of Maslow's hierarchy of needs, Kanfer (1992) suggests that there is now general agreement amongst researchers that there are five basic personality traits: neuroticism; extroversion; openness to experience; agreeableness; and conscientiousness. It is the last trait, conscientiousness, that has been most closely linked to volition and job performance. For example, Barrick and Mount (1991, p. 18) found that 'individuals who exhibit traits associated with a strong sense of purpose, obligation, and persistence generally perform better than those who do not'.

These findings are similar to those of another well-known theorist, David McClelland, who advanced the theory of achievement motivation (1971). McClelland distinguished between three types of needs: achievement, affiliation, and power. People with a high need for achievement were found to 'exhibit long-term involvement, competition against some standard of excellence, and unique accomplishment' (Hellriegel, Slocum and Woodman, 1995, p. 179). People with a high need for affiliation were found to 'establish, maintain, and restore close personal relationships with others', whereas people with a high need for power were found to 'take action that affects the actions of others' (Hellriegel *et al.*, 1995, p. 179). It is this type of dispositional research that has led many organizations to attempt to hire employees with the 'right' personality. In order to have highly motivated employees, employers endeavour to hire people with a high degree of conscientiousness, self-awareness, and a primary concern with task accomplishment. Large organizations may employ the services of a psychologist or consulting company to complete such assessments for them. Smaller organizations can conduct similar, although somewhat less precise, assessments through the use of appropriate interview questions.

Motive theories

Motive theories are concerned with the effect of environmental conditions on psychologically based motives (e.g. feelings of inequity, competence, satisfaction), which in turn affect behaviour. Motives can have both positive and negative effects. For example, feelings of inequity (e.g. a wage discrepancy) can be demotivating. Feelings of competence (e.g. being assigned a challenging task) can be motivating. Two areas of research that deal with these issues are *equity theory* (which deals with distributive and procedural justice) and *intrinsic motivation*.

Equity theory (Adams, 1963) is based on the premise that people want to be treated fairly and that when they are not, they seek to redress this imbalance. Equity is a particularly important principle in motivation research as 'feelings of unfairness' are one of the most commonly reported sources of job dissatisfaction (Hellriegel *et al.*, 1995, p. 193). Equity theory proposes how feelings of unfairness arise as well as how people respond to such feelings. Specifically, this theory suggests that individuals assign approximate values to their inputs for given tasks (e.g. ability, effort, skills). They also assign approximate values to the outcomes they receive for their inputs (e.g. financial rewards, recognition, future opportunities, enjoyment). They also compare outcome/input ratio to the outcome/input ratios of others who are engaged in similar work. If an inequity is identified, the individual will seek to restore balance by adjusting their inputs in the future.

As an illustration, can you recall a time when you worked very hard on an assignment for a course, while your classmate (of similar ability) did not? For some reason, you received similar grades. How did you feel? How did you respond? Equity theory suggests that you would have noticed this inequity and attempted to redress it. How might you have done so? Some students might have reconsidered their ratio assessment (e.g. they might have accepted the fact that their friend probably worked harder than they claimed). If you took this path, you probably decided to put forth a similar effort on your next assignment in the course. Other students might have concluded that in this situation outputs exist independently of inputs (i.e. regardless of your effort, you will receive a B). If you believe this to be true, you might reduce your inputs on future assignments in the hope of improving your input/output ratio. Lastly, some students might have decided to try even harder on the next assignment, in the hope that the increased output would more than compensate for any additional inputs.

In applying the concept of equity theory to the workplace, a number of scenarios come to mind. For example, equity theory helps explain why employees become demotivated when managers favour a select few, thereby contributing to the formation of a clique, for reasons unrelated to performance (e.g. giving them more attention, increased responsibility, preferred shifts or better rates of pay). Conversely, it explains why linking pay to performance (i.e. increasing someone's salary in return for superior performance) can be an effective motivator. In hospitality and tourism SMEs personal friendships between employees inevitably arise. Managers are well advised to maintain a friendly yet professional relationship with their staff.

Another interesting issue related to equity theory pertains to the employment of part-time workers, a common practice amongst many small to medium-sized hospitality organizations. A recent Canadian study found that the commitment of part-time workers to their jobs was equal to that of full-time workers when they were treated equitably. If this was not the case, their commitment was less:

> Organizations should be extremely aware of the importance and complexity of relative equity. Organizations need to recognize that job attitudes among part-timers depend a good deal on their perception of their treatment relative to that of full-time employees. Hence, there may be a real need to minimize overt differences in benefits and ... perhaps overt differences in supervision and treatment on the job. (Tansky, Gallagher and Wetzel, 1997, p. 324)

Equity theory also helps explain why employee sabotage (e.g. pilferage, absenteeism, poor quality work) is a common problem in SMEs where a proportion of jobs are low paid. Employees justify their behaviour on the basis of a perceived inequity between their efforts and outcomes. This is a very common problem. The American Management Association estimates that employee theft routinely costs US organizations more than US$10 billion a year (Hellriegel *et al.*, 1995, p. 196). In order to minimize such behaviour, some human resource managers develop well-structured compensation systems to ensure internal equity. They also routinely check and match the wages and benefits offered by their competitors. Human resource managers tend to share this type of information with one another as it contributes to the lowering of turnover across the board. Lastly, they should also endeavour to establish a fair minimum level of compensation to ensure that employees' basic needs are met.

Managers in hospitality and tourism SMEs should pay particular attention to issues of equity. It is common practice for managers to focus on improving profitability through the vigorous control of labour costs. While cost control can be a sound management practice, when taken to the extreme, productivity, quality, and long-term viability can suffer. For example, in a study of management practices in one large, US-based restaurant chain, managers were found to regularly engage in a number of highly questionable practices in order to reduce labour costs (Christensen Hughes, 1996). These practices included reducing staffing levels to the point where customer service levels were jeopardized; firing competent long-term staff and replacing them with less expensive new hires; delaying performance evaluations which, owing to company policy, would have resulted in pay increases; and failing to pay overtime (as required by law). Not surprisingly, this organization experienced declining customer service and product quality as well as high levels of employee dissatisfaction, turnover and employee sabotage.

Building further on the concept of equity theory, researchers have also pursued the concept of 'procedural justice'. Procedural justice pertains to 'perceptions about the organizational procedures used to make outcome decisions' (Kanfer, 1992, p. 17). Research has shown that when people are given the opportunity to participate in organizational processes such as performance evaluations or decisions that affect them, their perceptions of fairness increase, despite the actual outcomes received. This finding has resulted in the identification of five procedural justice norms (Fogler and Bies, 1989; Tyler and Bies, 1990):

- adequate consideration of an employee's viewpoint;
- suppression of personal bias;
- consistent application of criteria across employees;
- provision of timely feedback after a decision;
- provision of an adequate explanation for the decision to employees.

Research on the impact of procedural justice has shown that by adopting these norms, managers can have an indirect but positive impact on employee motivation. Managers who want to maintain a motivated work-force should endeavour to treat their employees fairly and involve them in decisions that concern them.

In addition to the concept of equity, many motivational researchers are interested in understanding the relative effects of *intrinsic* and *extrinsic* factors on employee motivation and performance. *Intrinsic* factors are defined as being related to the actual content of the job and include 'feelings of competence, achievement, responsibility, significance, importance, personal growth and meaningful contribution' (Beer, Spector, Lawrence, Quinn Mills, and Walton, 1985, p. 411). *Extrinsic* motivators are defined as being external to the job (e.g. wages, tips and fringe benefits – vacation pay, health plans, employee meals, staff parties, and access to leisure events). One of the best-known motivation theories that addresses the effects of extrinsic and intrinsic factors is Frederick Herzberg's motivator-hygiene theory. Herzberg, Mausner and Snyderman (1959) argued that extrinsic factors (or hygienes as he called them) can only lead to dissatisfaction (when they are insufficient). Intrinsic factors (or motivators) on the other hand can lead to satisfaction (when they are sufficient). In other words, according to Herzberg, paying an employee more money (an extrinsic factor) to do a job in which they are not interested (an intrinsic factor) may prevent them from feeling dissatisfied, but it will not increase their motivation for doing their best work. Based on this premise, managers should focus on designing jobs that employees find intrinsically rewarding and that meet their needs for self-determination.

Students often react to Herzberg's theory with disbelief. A common response is, 'But I find money very motivational!' To understand Herzberg's premise better imagine that you are given an assignment that you do not find at all appealing (e.g. to create a list of all the papers that have ever been written on motivation). You are confident that you have the ability to complete this task and that you will receive an adequate grade if you do. How motivated would you be to do your best work? If your teacher told you that your assigned grade would be inflated one level to compensate for the tedium of the task, would your level of motivation be any higher? Herzberg's point is that motivation is independent of the grade or extrinsic reward you are likely to receive. Should you get the higher grade you may feel less dissatisfied than you would have with the average grade, but in order for your level of motivation to increase (i.e. for you to be willing to do your best work), you probably would have needed a different assignment, one you found intrinsically motivating.

Despite the rationality of this argument, other researchers have found that extrinsic factors can in fact be motivating. One explanation for this is that extrinsic rewards can be linked to intrinsic rewards. For example, being well paid can help an employee feel valued, leading to feelings of competence and self-worth. Another explanation is that employees have different needs: employees operating at Maslow's lowest level may be motivated by extrinsic factors, while employees operating at Maslow's highest level may be motivated by intrinsic factors. Supporting this argument, Tansky *et al.* (1997) found that the relative importance of intrinsic versus extrinsic factors could be explained in part by age and part-time status. Given the high percentage of part-time students who work in the hospitality industry, this issue should be of particular concern. For example, students may perceive their part-time job as a temporary means of earning money and thus not be interested in a job that is intrinsically rewarding. Retirees who choose to work, but not for monetary reasons, may be very interested in a job that is intrinsically rewarding. Yet another argument pertains to culture. Adler and Graham (1989) found that for US workers, Herzberg's motivators accounted for 80 per cent of the factors that led to job satisfaction, while hygiene factors accounted for only 20 per cent. For workers in other countries these percentages varied. For example, for Finnish workers, motivators accounted for 90 per cent of the factors leading to job satisfaction. For Italian workers, motivators accounted for only 60 per cent.

Hersey and Blanchard (1969) provide a different perspective on extrinsic and intrinsic motivation. In 1946 they conducted a survey that asked employees about the importance of various job factors in 'motivating them,

Table 5.6 Comparison of employee responses

Factor	Year			
	1946	1980	1986	1992
Full appreciation of work done	1	2	2	2
Feeling of being in on things	2	3	3	9
Sympathetic help with personal problems	3	9	10	10
Job security	4	4	4	3
Good wages	5	5	5	1
Interesting work	6	1	1	5
Promotion and growth in the organization	7	6	6	4
Personal or company loyalty to employees	8	8	8	6
Good working conditions	9	7	7	7

as employees, to do their best work'. They found that 'appreciation of work done' was the most important motivational factor. This study was replicated in 1980, 1986 and 1992 (see Table 5.6 for cross-year comparisons). In both the 1980 and 1986 surveys 'interesting work' was the most important factor. By 1992, however, 'interesting work' had dropped to fifth place, while 'good wages' was ranked most important. What might account for these changes? Carol Wiley suggested that the rankings reflect what 'employees value but lack' (1997, p. 276). Based on this premise, in the 1940s employees lacked appreciation. By the 1980s employee appreciation programmes, although not always effectively implemented, had become relatively common. As a result, this need dropped from first to second place and employees began to seek increased fulfilment, self-expression and 'interesting work'. Economic instability in the late 1980s and early 1990s, however, resulted in a decline in the importance of 'interesting work' and a marked increase in the importance of basic needs such as 'good wages' and 'job security'; they had regressed to a lower level of need.

Today, the importance of intrinsic factors is reflected in almost every North American-based, management theory, in the form of, for example, participative management, empowerment, total quality management and re-engineering. Each of these theories incorporates elements of 'non-traditional work systems', which have been associated with positive organizational outcomes such as increased employee commitment, quality, productivity, and customer responsiveness. In contrast, 'traditional work systems' are often related to high rates of absenteeism and turnover, lack of worker commitment, poor product quality, inconsistent products, lack of organizational flexibility, and the need for increased levels of managerial

Table 5.7 Contrasting approaches to human resource management

Traditional work system	*Non-traditional work system*
• Narrowly defined jobs	• Broadly defined jobs
• Specialization of employees	• Rotation of employees through jobs
• Pay by specific job content	• Pay by skills mastered
• Evaluation by direct supervision	• Evaluation by peers
• Work is under close supervision	• Self- or peer-supervision
• Assignment of overtime or transfer by rule book	• Team assigns members to cover vacancies in flexible fashion
• No career development	• Concern for learning and growth
• Employees as individuals	• Employees in a team
• Employee is ignorant about business	• Team runs a business; business data shared widely
• Status symbols used to reinforce hierarchy	• Status differences minimized
• Employees have input on few matters	• Broad employee participation

Adapted from: Beer *et al.* (1985, p. 583)

control and supervision. It is interesting to note that both intrinsic and extrinsic factors are included in the list of non-traditional job factors shown in Table 5.7.

Writing on the link between non-traditional work system practices and motivation, Thomas and Velthouse (1990) consider that employees feel empowered when they have a sense of influence, competence and meaning-fulness in the workplace. Coleman (1996) agrees, adding that good employee performance results from a 'caring' management style. In other words, employees feel empowered when information, authority, resources and accountability are shared with them. Many principles listed in the non-traditional model have long been a part of management practice in hospital-ity and tourism SMEs. With fewer employees, broadly defined jobs and a sense of team-work have been essential attributes of organizational success. What is less common is the degree to which decision-making authority and responsibility have been shared with front-line employees. Some owners believe they alone must make decisions, and thus tightly monitor and control the activities of their employees. Others believe there are inherent benefits in involving employees at all levels in the decision-making process, and in treating their employees as partners in the enterprise.

Hospitality and tourism organizations of all sizes use a variety of extrinsic and intrinsic rewards for motivating their employees. For example, looking to several large American theme parks (Disneyland, Knott's Berry Farm and Universal Studios), a variety of special services, benefits and recognition programmes are offered (Jerome and Kleiner, 1995):

- special event tickets;
- theme park passes for friends and family;
- discounts on company merchandise;
- special previews and parties;
- sporting leagues and recreational programmes;
- service recognition awards;
- attendance awards;
- milestone awards.

Further, all three theme parks conduct annual employee surveys to analyse employee morale and satisfaction. When employees were recently asked at Disney, 'What would you work hard for?' the top three responses were:

- increased pay;
- recognition;
- additional involvement.

While smaller organizations may not have access to Disney's kind of facilities, they can achieve the same effect, albeit on a smaller scale. Special evenings where friends and relatives receive a special welcome; discounted meals and merchandise for employees; staff parties; sporting leagues; and fund-raising for charities are all common vehicles for building employee morale and team spirit. Employee awards, pay rises, promotions, and verbal support and encouragement can all be effective in fostering individual recognition: 'the key is not necessarily what recognition is bestowed, but the fact that the employee is being recognized' (Hopkins, 1995, p. 27). Or, as Wiley puts it, 'The need to feel appreciated is deeply ingrained in all employees .... Praise for a job well done is probably the most powerful, yet least costly and most underused, motivation tool' (1997, p. 275).

One cautionary note pertains to the serving of alcohol at staff functions. As with the discussion on equity theory, it is important for managers to comport themselves in a professional manner when in the company of employees. Over-indulgence in recreational drugs or alcohol at staff functions (on the part of employees and/or managers) can lead to many problems (e.g. liquor licence violations, sexual harassment charges, reduced productivity the next day), and should not be encouraged or condoned. This advice may be difficult for some managers to follow, given the nature of the working environment in many hospitality establishments. Management should openly discuss this issue amongst themselves and establish clear behavioural codes and policies.

In summary, as suggested by Herzberg *et al.* (1959), intrinsic factors can play a large role in motivation. Other researchers have argued that extrinsic rewards can also be important, depending upon employee age, part-time versus full-time status, cultural background, and current need level. Managers should endeavour to offer their employees both intrinsic and extrinsic rewards.

Cognitive choice

One of the best known cognitive choice theories is expectancy theory, which was first proposed by Victor Vroom (1964). Expectancy theory is based on four key assumptions (Hellriegel *et al.*, 1995, p. 188):

- people have expectations about their work which are shaped by a combination of personality and environmental factors;
- while at work, people regularly engage in conscious choice (e.g. whether to come to work, how hard to work, which tasks to prioritize);
- individuals have different needs and goals. Therefore, rewards associated with successful task completion will be valued differently, by different employees;
- individuals decide among alternative courses of behaviour, based on their perceptions of whether their behaviour/effort will lead to outcomes they desire.

Putting these assumptions together, expectancy theory suggests that people calculate the probability that if they expend effort they will be successful in completing the task (a first-level outcome). Next, they assess the strength of the relationship – or instrumentality – between first-level outcomes and second-level outcomes (that successful task accomplishment will lead to further rewards such as pay, promotion, attention, sense of accomplishment). Lastly, they assess their preference (valence) for the second-level outcomes. Taken together, these assessments determine the degree to which a person will be motivated to complete the task.

In applying these propositions to your experiences as a student, expectancy theory suggests that how hard you work on a given assignment is dependent upon:

- your perception that working hard will result in successful task completion (i.e. the completion of the assignment);

- your assessment of the instrumentality between assignment completion and other outcomes (i.e. a good grade, feelings of accomplishment, praise, passing the course);
- the valence or value you place on these second-level outcomes.

As with the other motivation theories reviewed, expectancy theory has its share of critics. Of particular concern is the extent to which expectancy theory assumes people's day-to-day behaviour is based on ongoing, thorough, conscious assessments of expectancy, instrumentality and valence (Landy and Becker, 1990). In response to these criticisms, Guest (1984) suggests that expectancy theory may only be appropriate for explaining major decisions for which several alternatives are clearly delineated and ample reflective time is available. Regardless, expectancy theory provides useful ideas for the workplace. As with the other theories, it suggests that managers should endeavour to identify the types of rewards their employees value. It also emphasizes the importance of explicitly making the link between first-level and second-level outcomes (e.g. 'The person who sells the most appetizers this week will get a $25 gift certificate'). Lastly, expectancy theory highlights the important role employee perceptions of the link between effort and performance play in motivation. Employees may perceive a poor link between effort and performance if work-loads are excessive; if they are poorly trained; or if they are given insufficient supplies, poor equipment, or confusing directions. If faced with poorly motivated employees, managers would be wise to give consideration to such factors. Regularly scheduled meetings with employees (either in a group or one-on-one) can help managers identify such problems before they get out of hand. Open door policies and suggestion programmes can also be useful in getting employee input. As with all employee participation programs, management must truly want such input and be willing to respond to suggestions they receive in order for the programme to work.

Proximal constructs

As previously stated, proximal constructs have a direct impact on performance. Kanfer's (1992) framework identifies goal-setting (Locke, 1968) as a major theoretical contribution to this area.

Goal-setting theory

Goal-setting theory is based on the notion that when people are given and accept difficult and specific goals, they out-perform people who are simply told 'do your best' (Kanfer, 1992). This effect on performance is thought to occur through the direct impact of goals on employee behaviour in four specific areas: attention/direction, effort/intensity, persistence and strategy development. Unlike the distal theories reviewed, empirical support for Locke's propositions has been substantial (Kanfer, 1992). Building on Locke's work, researchers have found that the impact of goals on perform-ance is further strengthened through positive feedback (Kanfer, 1992). Attention has also been given to the effect of the goal-setting process itself. When employees play a role in establishing their own goals, or when it is explained to them why a particular goal is important, goal commitment and performance are further enhanced.

Lastly, the work of Albert Bandura (1977, 1986) on self-efficacy has implications for goal-setting theory. Bandura defined self-efficacy as the belief in one's capabilities to mobilize the motivation, cognitive resources and courses of action needed to meet given situational demands. Bandura, in drawing attention to organizational constraints (as in expectancy theory), cautioned that goal setting and self-efficacy are not necessarily sufficient conditions for employee performance:

> Efficacious artisans and athletes cannot perform well with faulty equipment and efficacious executives cannot put their talents to good use if they lack adequate financial and material resources ... When performances are impeded by disin-centives, inadequate resources, or external constraints, self-judged efficacy will exceed the actual performance. (Bandura, 1986, p. 396)

Bandura (1986, p. 348) also wrote on the importance of rewards and of subordinate identification with organizational and task goals; he com-mented that 'there are many things that people can do with certainty of success that they do not perform because they have no incentives to do so', and that 'people do not care much how they do in activities that have little or no significance for them, and they expend little effort on devalued activities'. In support of these statements Bandura (1986) also cites labora-tory studies in which people were paid to sacrifice quality for quantity. He found that people who subscribed to high standards continued to strive for quality despite personal financial disincentives to do so.

The implications of goal setting theory for managers include: the import-ance of establishing challenging goals; the necessity of clearly communicating the importance of assigned goals; the need for participative goal-setting procedures; and the need to identify and minimize organizational constraints.

SUMMARY

In summary, several models of motivation have been reviewed. No single theory tells the whole story; all have some value. Despite their distinct differences, some common themes can be identified. These are summarized in Table 5.8.

Table 5.8 The **ALERT** motivational model

A Managers must be **AWARE** of their employees' needs. This can be achieved through surveys, conversation and observation.
L Managers must **LISTEN** to their employees. This will help identify needs as well as organizational barriers to need satisfaction. Through being listened to, employees' intrinsic needs for involvement may be met.
E Managers must make their **EXPECTATIONS** known. If performance expectations are not made explicit, employees will likely fail to meet them. When employees are involved in establishing goals or expectations, or at least understand the importance of them, they will be more committed. Managers can further reinforce expectations through feedback after task completion.
R Managers must offer their employees both intrinsic and extrinsic **REWARDS.** Rewards should be equitable (both internally and externally), clearly linked to task performance (i.e. have high instrumentality), be valued (i.e. be of high valence), and sufficient (i.e. allow basic needs to be met). Extrinsic rewards should be supported by appropriate compensation systems. Intrinsic rewards should be supported through job design, philosophies of empowerment, and employee recognition programmes.
T Managers must provide adequate **TOOLS** and **TRAINING.** Without adequate tools and training employees will perceive a lack of connection between effort and performance, and effort will eventually diminish.

CONCLUSION

In conclusion, the motivational literature is rich with suggestions for how managers might best motivate their employees. Managers must be aware of the needs of their employees and should design jobs, policies and systems that will help their employees' needs to be met. Managers need to be particularly aware of individual differences such as age, part-time versus full-time status, and cultural background, since all can affect employee needs. To accommodate this diversity, managers may want to use many of the approaches that have been identified throughout this chapter and summarized in the ALERT Motivational Model in Table 5.8.

REFERENCES

Adams, J. (1963), Toward an understanding of inequity. *Journal of Abnormal and Social Psychology*, **67**, 422–36.

Adler, N. and Graham, J. (1989), Cross-cultural interaction: the international comparison fallacy. *Journal of International Business Studies*, **20**, 515–37.

Alderfer, C. (1972), *Existence, Relatedness and Growth: Human Needs in Organizational Settings*. New York: Free Press.

Bandura, A. (1977), Self-efficacy: toward a unifying theory of behavioral change, *Psychological Review*, **84**(2), 191–215.

Bandura, A. (1986), *Social Foundations of Thought and Action: A Social-Cognitive View*. Englewood Cliffs, NJ: Prentice Hall.

Barrick, M. and Mount, M. (1991), The big five personality dimensions and job performance: a meta-analysis. *Personnel Psychology*, **44**, 1–26.

Beer, M., Spector, B., Lawrence, P., Quinn Mills, D. and Walton, R. (1985), *Human Resource Management: A General Manager's Perspective*. New York, NY: Free Press.

Campbell, J. and Pritchard, R. (1976), Motivation theory in industrial and organizational psychology. In M. D. Dunette (ed.), *Handbook of Industrial and Organizational Psychology*. Chicago: Rand-McNally, pp. 63–130.

Christensen Hughes, J. (1996), Beyond rhetoric: an in-depth account of one organization's experience with empowerment. PhD Dissertation, York University.

Coleman, H. (1996), Why employee empowerment is not just a fad. *Leadership and Organization Development Journal*, **17**(4), 29–36.

Deci, E. and Ryan, R. (1980), The empirical exploration of intrinsic motivational processes. In L. Berkowitz (ed.), *Advances in Experimental Social Psychology*, 13. New York: Academic Press, pp. 39–80.

Fogler, R. and Bies, R. (1989), Managerial responsibilities and procedural justice. *Employee Responsibilities and Rights Journal*, **2**, 79–80.

Gomez-Mejia, L., Balkin, D., Cardy, R. and Dimick, D. (1997), *Managing Human Resources*. Scarborough, ON: Prentice Hall Canada.

Guest, D. (1984), What's new in motivation. *Personnel Management*, May, 20–3.

Hackman, J. and Oldham, G. (1976), Motivation through the design of work: test of a theory. *Organizational Behavior and Human Performance*, **16**, 250–79.

Hellriegel, D., Slocum, J. and Woodman, R. (1995), *Organizational Behaviour*, 7th edn, St. Paul, MN: West Publishing Company.

Hersey, P. and Blanchard, K. (1969), *Management of Organizational Behaviour*. Englewood Cliffs, NJ: Prentice Hall.

Herzberg, F., Mausner, B. and Snyderman, B. (1959), *The Motivation to Work*. New York: John Wiley & Sons.

Hofstede, G. (1984), *Culture's Consequences*. Newbury Park, CA: Sage Publications.

Hopkins, H. (1995), A challenge to managers: five ways to improve employee morale. *Executive Development*, **8**(7), 26–8.

Jerome, L. and Kleiner, B. (1995), Employee morale and its impact on service: what companies do to create a positive service experience. *Managing Service Quality*, **5**(6), 21–5.

Kanfer, R. (1992), Work motivation: new directions in theory and research. *International Review of Industrial and Organization Psychology*, **7**, 1–53.

Landy, F. and Becker, W. (1990), Motivation theory reconsidered. In B. M. Staw, and L. L. Cummings (eds), *Work in Organizations*. Greenwich, CT and London: JAI Press, pp. 1–38.

Locke, E. (1968), Toward a theory of task motivation and incentives. *Organizational Behavior and Human Performance*, **3**, 157–89.

Locke, E. and Henne, D. (1986), Work motivation theories. *International Review of Industrial and Organizational Psychology*, 1–7.

Locke, E., Shaw, K., Saari, L. M. and Latham, G. (1981), Goal setting and task performances: 1969–1980. *Psychological Bulletin*, **90**, 125–52.

Maslow, A. (1954), *Motivation and Personality*. New York: Harper & Row.

Maslow, A. (1965), *Eupsychian Management*. Homewood, II: Dorsey Press.

McClelland, D. (1971), *Motivational Trends in Society*. Morristown, NJ: General Learning Press.

Oxford American Dictionary (1980), Edited by E. Ehrlich, S. Berg Flexner, G. Carruth, and J. Hawkins, New York: Oxford University Press.

Schaffer, R. (1953), Job satisfaction as related to need satisfaction in work. *Psychological Monographs*, **67**, 304.

Tansky, J., Gallagher, D. and Wetzel, K. (1997), The effect of demographics, work status, and relative equity on organizational commitment: looking among part-time workers. *Canadian Journal of Administrative Sciences*, **14**(3), 315–26.

Thomas, K. S. and Velthouse, B. A. (1990), Cognitive elements of empowerment: an 'interpretive' model of intrinsic task motivation. *Academy of Management Review*, **15**(4), 666–81.

Tyler, T. and Bies, R. (1990), Beyond formal procedures: the interpersonal context of procedural justice. In J. Carroll (ed.), *Applied Social Psychology and Organizational Settings*. Hillsdale, NJ: Lawrence Erlbaum, pp. 77–98.

Vroom, V. (1964), *Work and Motivation*. New York: Wiley & Sons.

Wiley, C. (1997), What motivates employees according to over 40 years of motivation surveys. *International Journal of Manpower*, **18**(3), 263–80.

CHAPTER SIX

Information Technology for Human Resources

Bonnie Farber Canziani

INTRODUCTION

Most competitive hospitality organizations today are taking advantage of the many options for automating some or all of the functions of human resources (HR). The answer to the question of where and how to automate HR is usually dependent on the needs of the specific hospitality company that is exploring information system solutions. Small hospitality companies may have different needs and budgets from very large national or international chains. Some companies are looking for a total human resource information system (HRIS), while others are content to automate only easily captured functions such as payroll or stock plans. Other companies are making choices between client/server and individual stand-alone PC setups. Still others are looking at the Internet as a critical resource for their company. Often, a technology champion appears in the ranks of HR management in a company, and proceeds to advance the company's learning curve in the use of HR technology solutions.

The information presented in this chapter offers a systematic exploration of the use of information systems and technology in the area of human resources in small to medium-sized hospitality companies. For the benefit of a novice reader, technical terms are defined within the context of the chapter. The presumption is that the reader needs only a basic understanding of the concepts of information systems and their use in business functional areas. This chapter may essentially serve as a primary reading on the usefulness of technologically based software systems and the Internet for the efficient and effective delivery of human resources services to a hospitality company.

Table 6.1 Sample cost items in an HRIS system

Cost category	Sample cost items
HR application software	Off the shelf HR functional software
	Customized HR programs
Operations software	Operating systems
	Database management system
	Data collection and transfer tools
Hardware	Dedicated servers
	New user workstations
	User workstation upgrades
Telecommunications	Local area networks (LAN)
	Wide area networks (WAN)
	Utility service and labour
Implementation resources	Internal information system support
	Contract or license system support
	Independent consultant agreements
Training	General system managers
	Database administrators
	HR applications users
	Information end-users

HOW DOES AN HRIS ADD VALUE TO AN ORGANIZATION?

According to Richards-Carpenter (1997) the *1997 Computers in Personnel and Training Survey* revealed that 22 per cent of all HRISs purchased by respondents by the time of the study were not yet one year old, and 40 per cent of systems purchased were between one and two years old. Several reasons surfaced as the primary drivers of new system purchases by HR managers: to increase the quality of general reporting (96 per cent), to facilitate business re-engineering and cost-efficiency (85 per cent), to devolve HR responsibilities (75 per cent), to access the Internet (71 per cent) and to integrate the HR system with payroll (70 per cent). Typical costs involved in procuring and using an HRIS relate to hardware, software and implementation expenses. Included in a preliminary budget proposal are such cost items (Minneman, 1996) as depicted in Table 6.1. In proposing any outlay of capital, the HR manager must clarify for upper management the expected benefits of using an HRIS. The HR manager must show how the system will allow the company to leverage the human resources investment in a way that will enable the company to respond to HR needs and challenges efficiently and effectively in a timely manner. HR managers will be expected to quantify anticipated benefits from the new HRIS in order to justify the substantial requested investment in the HR system infrastructure. Many HR managers trying to justify this expenditure focus on reducing organizational expenses: they ask how the new technology can perform current HR tasks at a lower cost. For example, the automated functions of many HR software packages eliminate manual administrative processes such as monitoring employee bonuses for referrals that are subsequently hired, or submitting paperwork to obtain employee identification cards or building passes.

Also, information kiosks for employee self-service investigation of HR information sources can even reduce the number of clerical personnel needed to answer employee inquiries. Having all of the employee data – name, age, date employment began, disability, and health and salary information – in one location makes accessibility quick and easy. For example, Samuel Greengard Workforce (1998) states that:

> Processes that used to take two or three days now are completed in a few hours. Across the entire department, about 10 per cent of HR's work now is transactional in nature, compared to 60 per cent to 70 per cent only two years ago. . . . In most cases, the return is approximately [US]$35 to [US]$50 per employee per year at a large company and as much as [US]$100 per employee annually at a small firm.

Greengard (1998a) considers that it is advantageous for companies to use technology to its full advantage. Two more strategic approaches documenting the anticipated benefits of purchasing and implementing HRIS have been suggested in the HRIS literature: Sanders' 'targets of opportunity' (Sunoo, 1995) and the 'value-added approach'.

Sanders (Sunoo, 1995) speaks of seven 'targets of opportunity' or areas where there is the most potential to improve the HR function through the use of information technology:

- *speed* handling vast quantities of data quickly and efficiently;
- *accuracy* reducing the propensity of human error involved in data handling;
- *memory* maintaining and rapidly accessing historical files;
- *comprehensiveness* automating a wide array of HR functions;
- *availability* making information available to more users in departments in and outside HR;

- *objectivity* increasing the use of factual or objective data in decisions related to employees;
- *economy* reducing the operational and paperwork costs associated with HR.

Human resource managers should clarify what benefits they would expect from a new HRIS in each of the seven areas. In addition, installing a new HRIS can be co-ordinated with a redesign of HR processes to streamline activities in a beneficial way for the company.

Another approach for justifying the purchase of HR technology requires the HR manager to think in business terms and to find out how a new or upgraded HRIS will help the organization better deploy workforce resources in meeting its company goals. This second approach for justifying an investment in technology uses a cost–benefit or value-added perspective. The purchase of system components is justified on the basis of the contributions they make to company business goals, and not merely on the basis of purchase price or paperwork cost reduction.

The ideal HRIS proposal identifies the vital role of HR in advancing information-supported solutions to the employment of personnel, worker and organizational development, performance management, and other internal challenges. Human resource managers need to recognize their department's strategic role as provider of internal services such as job definition, recruitment, orientation, training and development, recognition and reward, performance assessment, and progressive discipline. In essence, this value-added approach turns the HRIS into a potential critical success factor for the company by defining the business value of employee-related information. Managers developing a time-line for automating different areas of HR should also advocate implementing first those functions and features that provide the greatest business impact for the company.

As we have suggested, HR activities support key business goals of a company. These company goals often appear in an organizational mission statement. Specific goals may take the form of planned company movement into new geographic areas or tourism markets; new uses of operational technology; or planned growth by merger and acquisition of similar or related service businesses. The human resources department has a fundamental responsibility to ensure that company units undergoing these changes have access to the right sets of employee skills when needed, and that employees are informed and supported as their operational departments implement changes in focus and in work processes. Human resource strategy must ensure that information technology is used to help line managers make decisions through supporting managers' access to and analysis of employee data. This type of decision support to operational managers may be realized by extending traditionally centralized mainframe HR capacities to managerial end-users through local area networks supporting a more decentralized and user-friendly PC environment.

HR FUNCTIONS SUPPORTED BY HRIS

Historical stages of HRIS development

Historically, automated personnel systems were designed to store large quantities of employee and company data in flat files that could be printed out in columns, and perhaps sorted and/or subtotalled. These first systems were generally unable to perform complex data analyses to answer real-life business questions about the use of human resources. The costs of designing applications programs for early systems were simply too high, and most systems were controlled by computer technicians and database administrators who were overloaded just keeping up with the technical difficulties arising in inputting data and maintaining system viability. Small businesses did not typically invest during the earliest phase of HRIS development because they could not see benefits: the quantity of data they typically processed was small. Many small and medium-sized hospitality companies that are now moving to an HRIS have been the last die-hards to give up paper-based filing systems.

Over time, automated personnel systems have become more user friendly, and hardware and software faster and cheaper. HR professionals have, across the hospitality field, slowly developed expertise in the use of applications software for a limited number of HR functions (e.g. payroll, benefits, and equal employment opportunities/affirmative action statistics). These professionals have begun to view the management and analysis of the automated database as *their* job rather than the job of a database technician. Today the HR professional in the hospitality industry is bombarded by software opportunities calling for the automation of some aspect of every important function in the human resources field. Many companies, however, still restrict access and control of the systems to a centralized HR information specialist, or, alternatively, disseminate HR department information formally to line managers and employees on a request for information basis. From a control standpoint, any use of and changes in the functions of the HRIS are in most cases decided by a centralized person or team residing in the HR area and seldom by the line managers needing the data. This leads to an observation that this centralization of control over the use of HRIS may have to be revisited at some point in the future. The next emerging goal of HRIS technology will likely be to extend access to human resources data beyond the HR department to line managers and employees themselves. For example, managers could see summaries of information about staff absence, for instance, and could look for further details and detect patterns. Employees could have direct access to sections of the system to fill in time-sheets, ask for holidays and e-mail requests to their line managers to be approved by electronic signature.

A corollary technological advancement is the use of the Internet and intranets to perform HR functions easily across great distances. According to Greengard (1997), the world-wide web has led to dramatic changes for HR. It is allowing corporations to recruit and provide information directly to students and professionals 24 hours a day. Curricula vitae can be processed automatically and fed into databases. Managers with vacancies can perform keyword searches among the candidates on file. Human resource managers who learn how the Internet works and how their companies can use it to maximum advantage will be the winners in the days ahead. The next section will provide examples of different applications of technology to HR.

Case examples: automated solutions to HR challenges

Recruitment

> Touted as 'Canada's greatest outdoor event', the Calgary Stampede is a unique HR challenge based on the influx of employees required during the 10-day July event. Although about 230 full time people are employed year round, this number increases by another 3000 during the Stampede itself. Before using an HRIS, the Calgary Stampede relied on a makeshift database system that Lorie Potter, HR Administrator, described as 'a fine system if all you needed to keep track of is a Christmas card mailing list – but, we have grown much bigger than this'. Not only does the Calgary Stampede need a flexible HRIS that will track thousands of employees, but one that can document the type of employment, whether it is full time or part time, year-round or event season only.
>
> To fill the 3000 positions that arise during the Stampede, the HR department both hosts a job fair and invites successful past employees to reapply. The job fair draws thousands of interested applicants each year. Certainly, organizing and later accessing appropriate applicant information could be a daunting task.

Once each applicant's demographic data is entered into the Stampede's HRIS, the HR department is granted quick and easy access to lists of applicant information based on parameters such as: positions available, interview scheduling, and applicant suitability.

In addition to the job fair, approximately 1800 letters are sent to past employees, inviting them to reapply. Each employee, past and present, has a custom-made file in the software program, showing their employment history, their rating (whether they are worth rehiring), and if they are currently employed by the Stampede. From here, a simple mail merge with an invitation letter results in 1800 invitations. Potter says, 'The old system required 20 hours of physically checking the present staff list, to make sure that invitations weren't being sent to individuals who stayed on as full time staff once the Stampede finished.' The HRIS solution chosen by the Stampede enables this world class rodeo to maximize efficiency. (Anon, 1997)

Performance appraisal

One small transit company with which the author has been involved is going on-line with a performance management system based on competency that close to 90 managers and supervisors will use to track performance of an estimated 1000 persons. Using screens of performance data available through an intranet, supervisors will be setting developmental goals for their employees in order to guide and motivate the employees to achieve increased performance success. The use of 360 degree performance appraisal will also be linked to this performance management system, so that multiple evaluations can be requested and reviewed online by employees. The need to computerize the process soon became evident because of an in-house policy on scheduling bus operators: at least twice a year more than 600 employees bid on new schedules, and, with their schedule changes, are commonly reassigned to different supervisors. Employee files then go to the next supervisor for continued observation of employee performance. Having the employee files on-line is expected to make completion and exchange of paper appraisal forms among supervisors a thing of the past. Managers will be able to spend more time ensuring that feedback is constructive and that goals set with the employee during the last supervisor's shift are monitored by the next supervisor. Instead of digging among forms in a paper folder, supervisors will be able to view screens of data that will let them know immediately what the employees have done during the intervening time since the last appraisal.

Internet recruitment

Many organizations use sites like E.Span, The Monster Board and Career Mosaic to complement existing recruiting strategies because general sites inexpensively and effectively post positions and trawl for resumés. Whereas the Sunday classifieds of the Los Angeles Times or Washington Post can run [US]$1000 or more per listing, the price online usually costs around [US]$100 per month, per posting. Also, the Internet helps companies connect with potential employees. Says Pamela James, senior staffing director at Irvine, California-based Taco Bell Corp.: 'The Web can extend your reach to people who didn't know about you or wouldn't normally think about you. It can help you find high quality applicants who almost certainly would have gone elsewhere.' (Greengard, 1998b)

TECHNICAL ISSUES IN THE DESIGN OF AN HRIS

From a technical standpoint, there are a number of critical factors to be evaluated in both existing (if any) and planned HR systems. Minimally, these factors include the preferred system environment; the operating systems in place or desired; database issues; and communications applications such as e-mail and the Internet.

System environment

One major consideration in the design of an HRIS is the choice of system environment. Three alternatives are available to HR departments: systems with limited function end-user terminals; server(s) with client workstations; and complete stand-alone workstation configurations. In the first set-up a server is structured as a central repository of operating programs, applications software and data; few or many end-user terminals or kiosks provide only limited input or read-only access to the end-users of the system. Individual HR employees or non-HR managers would tend to have less interaction with the system design or data. They would most likely receive pre-defined hard copy or computer screen reports providing data for regularly scheduled, routine decision-making that concerned employee issues. The other end of the spectrum is the stand-alone workstation configuration. This approach would provide a workstation complete with HR software and employee data to employees involved in company decision-making concerning HR information. These end-users (workstation owners) would have reasonable autonomy over the use of the HR software applications and data relevant to their job responsibilities. In this case workstations could be dedicated to support individual job functions of the HR employee, such as payroll or recruitment. Unfortunately, any arising need for sharing data among employees is satisfied solely by installing identical software on each end-user's system and by exchanging data manually (for example, by sharing diskettes). And again, line managers will have to request reports and analyses through the normal HR bureaucracy, and the HR employee will do most of the analysis and provide the reports in written form to the line manager requesting the information. The system environment that provides greater flexibility and access, while still ensuring some centralized control of system components and employee data is the client/server design. In this configuration, a central server is linked to client or HR employee workstations and carries the bulk of the HR applications software and employee data. However, employees can install additional business applications on their computers as needed; typically these latter applications are useful only to that employee and not to the other members of the company. More importantly, the HR department can install reporting and analytical tools into computers used by company executives and managers, who can then perform their own timely, customized analyses and then click and drag results right into report templates. Lastly, sharing of information or data across the linked client workstations is facilitated by updated telecommunication technologies, which also support electronic mail functions and internet web pages.

In general, smaller hospitality companies (fewer than five HR staff members) opt for one or a few independent workstations as they move into the technology arena. If the company is medium-sized or grows to have multiple staff in areas such as compensation or recruitment, the need for shared data increases and then a client/server approach best meets its needs.

Operating system

Two requirements need to be considered with respect to the operating system. First, that the HR application software will be compatible with certain brands of operating system software, e.g. Macintosh, Windows, Unix, or OS/2. In addition, the hospitality company must clarify which way it wants to go – match the current operating system or change to an operating system that supports the desired application software. Second, the most current version of the operating system, e.g. Windows 3.1, Windows 95 or Windows NT, will more than likely be needed to support the

HR software which will require some expense if the company is not yet in possession of it. Companies that have considerable investment or expertise in one brand of the operating system should focus on HR software that works with that operating system; it may be that only a version upgrade is required to get the HR system up and running.

Database

Application software purchased with the intent of automating specific HR functions may or may not include database functions within their capabilities. Some HR applications' products are expected to be compatible with, and extract relevant data from, an already existing database. Other products are based on relational databases such as FoxBase and Access. The relational type of database moves way beyond the simple sorting and sub-totalling of columns of data to supporting complex examinations of critical questions by looking at correlations among different types of company and employee data. For example, relational systems could conceivably track the dollar rises last year by employee classification and by department, and compare each of these categories across geographic locations.

Where possible, the product chosen should allow the user to customize fields, screens and relationships of data and to retain these user-specific parameters when the user installs software upgrades issued by the vendor. A small hospitality company may be more interested in eliminating unwanted fields or screens from the vendor's design, since the company may not need all the functions generally important to employers of numerous personnel. A case in point would be the training function. A small company may want to document a limited set of data, such as which workshop an employee attended on which date, but may have no real need to support a training registration process, e.g. trainee rosters, since all workshops are contracted off-site. The system needs analysis also should take into consideration the costs of data management and transfer, since it is more than likely that the company already has a computer database set up. For small companies, a software product that combines both functional and database procedures would be optimal since one HR employee most likely can manage both data management and data analysis functions. The cost of transferring existing employee data into the new software's database would be relatively low in a small company with few employees. Also, the HR employee would need to contract with or call only one vendor's technical support service in case of difficulties with the product.

Communication

Telecommunication services and infrastructure will be necessary to support intranet and Internet usage, including the maintenance of e-mail service and web sites. Web technology is inexpensive. The basic system configuration comprises a server hardware platform/operating system and WWW (world-wide web) server software. On the user side, employees need an inexpensive browser to navigate the information. Employees use hypertext links to search for and access text, graphics, audio or video, all of which are organized into home pages. At the basic level, this means that companies can do away with many costly corporate documents that are now produced on paper, such as human resources guides, newsletters, annual reports, maps, company facilities, price lists and product information.

Data protection

Laws on data security are emerging in most countries where electronic data transfer of information is commonplace. Human resource professionals are accustomed to protecting the privacy of their employees' personal information, and need to extend that commitment to information handled electronically. The Institute of Personnel and Development in the UK has devised a set of basic principles (IPD, 1996) that aims to:

• provide a policy framework of best practice for handling employee data;
• outline the legal obligations of personnel practitioners;
• seek to ensure consistency in the treatment of all data;
• outline the need for confidentiality and sensitivity;
• list the rights of employees;
• give guidance in information provision.

A code of ethics for HR is commendable, but concrete technical solutions to the issue of data security, involving multi-level passwords, administrative codes and system barriers, will need to be devised by the technical expert supporting the HRIS and other automated systems in the hospitality company.

Since the technical side of the HRIS purchase is the most unfamiliar for the majority of HR generalists, it is advisable to seek the counsel of an information technology (IT) expert before committing resources to a specific product. Small or medium-sized hospitality companies that do not retain an in-house IT specialist would do well to employ an IT consultant to help them think through their current and planned technical issues.

SEARCHING FOR AN HRIS SYSTEM

The software evaluation process

According to the *1997 Computers in Personnel and Training Survey*, the increasing array of automated HR systems available on the market has made the HRIS selection decision increasingly difficult (Richards-Carpenter, 1997). Given that there are more than 50 major HRISs available on the US market, and 48 vendors identified in a 1997 British HRIS exhibition, the search for the right system for a small or medium-sized hospitality company needs to be managed so that the selection process does not in itself become an impossible task. One rule of thumb according to Baker (1997) is to keep the vendor finalist list to a reasonable number of competing vendors – usually under five – for a more detailed comparison and evaluation. This goal is achieved more easily by observing the following best practices (Baker, 1997) in searching for and selecting an HRIS system.

Step 1 Identify the functional, technical and data requirements desired in the HR system. Make a wish list that labels features from a 'nice to have' up to 'absolute must for the company to achieve its goals'.

Step 2 Send out a request for information (RFI) to vendors. The RFI should describe the company's most essential functions and technical requirements, and is used to request that qualified vendors provide critical information about their products.

Step 3 Selectively reject vendor products that do not meet absolute or basic requirements. Systems that meet company needs with little or no customization will be less costly than those that need major modifications owing to lack of particular functions or incompatibility with current operating systems.

Step 4 Next, provide final candidates with a list of your functional requirements (see Appendix on pages 194–6) and request more detail on how their products match the needs of the company. Invite a select few to demonstrate their products and seek their technical solutions to any company-specific or uncommon needs, e.g. employees transfer regularly from one geographic location to another.

Step 5 Base the final decision on sound cost–benefit analysis. This applies to both small and large companies. Price is only one attribute, and even for small hospitality companies should not be the only driver of the purchase decision. Remember to evaluate the supplier as well as the product, since most HRISs need continual upgrading and service support to adapt to changing needs.

As noted earlier in this chapter, the proposed HRIS design for a company should specify the HR functions and reports that are most critical to the business goals of the company. Only then does it make sense to engage the company in an HR system selection process. The appendix (on pages 194–6) offers a comprehensive checklist for companies beginning the job of comparing and contrasting various system solutions for their human resources area. This appendix lists technical, functional and data requirements that represent the needs most commonly expressed by major business companies. Small and medium-sized companies can use this list in the context of their own budgets, employee policies and programmes, and HR direction.

Small to medium-sized hospitality organizations (with an HR department of fewer than five people) should consider systems that are cost-effective yet permit strategic management and employment of personnel. Critical cost reduction and value enhancement objectives can be met by automating attendance records, benefits and compensation, recruiting employee skills tracking, and payroll. Smaller companies will want a system that can grow with their business and should choose one that is relatively easy to run with minimal support or training costs that would add to the expense of using technology. Some examples of US-based software products for small companies include Benefits Xtra, HROffice, UltriPro for Windows, ABRA People Manager, People-Trak LT, HR Task Counselor, and HRTrack. The solution should be intuitive enough to use so that the people that need to use it can do so without extensive training. A common pitfall that occurs with smaller companies is that they overestimate their needs and implement an overly complex solution. The time and money spent implementing, learning and using these systems end up being a costly expense that could have been avoided with more realistic needs assessment.

As a company grows in number of personnel and of HR employees, it will be able to take advantage of some of the more sophisticated off-the-shelf products that encompass many of the functions listed in the product comparison sheets in the appendix (pages 194–6). In addition, most of the HRIS packages can be customized to provide flexibility in both report generation, and data collection and analysis. However, the high cost of custom solutions is usually prohibitive for smaller companies. Typically, the implementation time for an off-the-shelf solution can be as little as one-third the time of a custom solution. Several resources are available to start off the product search process:

- a Ziff-Davis CD–ROM called *Computer Select* (see http://www.(erc.nasa. gov/WWW/VCIM/cdroms.html), which contains digital computer magazines, including *PC Week, CIO,* and *Software* magazines. A company can scan the CD to peruse articles and ads on various HR software companies;
- the *Advanced Personnel System*, a census of software vendors to determine product features and functionality of their systems;
- an annual software buyers' guide provided by *HRMagazine*;
- additional websites including those of *HRWORLD* (http://www. hrworld.com/index.htm) and *The HR and Survey Software Page* (http:// www.cam.org/~steinbg/).

Outsourcing HR functions

Some small hospitality companies choose the route of outsourcing a portion of their HR functions. Of course, this option should be examined with the same rigour as the selection of an in-house system. Greengard (1997) suggests that outsourcing payroll has become immensely popular over the last few years. For many small and medium-sized companies, service bureaux are convenient and far less expensive. There is no need to invest in piles of hardware and software, and it is not necessary to learn new systems or provide training. One company is developing a benefits administration service using the net. Companies with 25 to 2000 employees or more can zap data to *Employease, Inc.* which handles, among other things, the processing of monthly invoices and generates enrolment forms and annual benefits statements.

BEYOND THE COMPANY HRIS

The impact of technology on the HR field

At least four major changes, all due to the influence of technological innovation, have occurred in the field of HR itself, beyond the obvious one of paperwork reduction. First, the HR generalist has joined the ranks of business employees who have been pushed and pulled into the domain of information technology, and been required to gain skills and knowledge that probably did not accompany their initial training in the personnel fields. A recent survey of senior human resources management in Canada shows that almost 75 per cent of the department's time is spent on low value-added administration. The main challenges cited were access to the information required for decisions, and the effort needed to gather data for reports.

Flynn (1995) provides another perspective on how the proactive HR professional will consider technology an ally in getting work done more efficiently – a particularly important point in an age where all functions are pushed to do more with less. Since the top leaders of companies are using technology in their domains, the HR manager who stays behind will be competitively disadvantaged. Flynn suggests that HR professionals will have to be techno-literate for their own sake and that of their employees. Human resource professionals must embrace technology and provide guidelines and support for employees; for example, employees need to be trained in computer skills, new time-management skills, and so on. Second, the HR specialist has seen a lessening of his/her autonomy over specific employee data and analytical techniques, since other company managers are clamouring to have access to more detailed analyses, and even want to do it themselves. By allowing managers and other non-HR staff members to access employee data directly from terminals or via data transfer into their personal computers, HR can shift some of the responsibility for strategic analysis of human resources cost and use to the department heads who manage these employees. These managers can move closer to their true sources of labour expense, and clarify the best scenarios for optimizing salary decisions and use of technical skills in their offices or shops. Third, companies have achieved a wider geographical perspective in HR recruitment and management through the availability of the Internet and e-mail. The Internet is enabling HR managers to engage in technologically supported activities such as local and wide area on-line recruiting and information dissemination. Fourth, employees have been given the opportunity to access needed information via kiosks or terminals without having to go through numerous paper barriers. In addition to self-service functions for managers, employee activities such as training are continuing to go on-line. Software products for a wide array of training topics are now available with sound, graphics and full-motion video. Self-paced just-in-time instruction will at least complement, if not replace entirely, traditional classroom training. The scheduling of employees and instructors during a fixed time period in a fixed place may be a thing of the past.

It has been suggested that eight powerful forces with implications for the use of technology at work impact employees in today's world:

1. as individuals we are learning to take more control of the things that affect us;
2. we are getting more comfortable interfacing with devices, many of which have a computer imbedded in them;
3. we are coming to expect and use services that operate continuously;
4. we are learning how to obtain comparative information that allows us to make better decisions;
5. we are less afraid of using technology to help us make critical decisions that affect our lives;
6. we expect assurances that the transactions we initiate are correct, that they can be reversed if necessary, and that we can receive feedback about them;
7. we demand speed: we dislike waiting for a system to download the next input or for a transaction to take an inordinate amount of time;
8. we can, when necessary, reach out and interact with the highest authority in a company providing a particular service. (Anon, 1996)

All in all the HR world of the future is an exciting one for the hospitality industry. Companies at all levels of the industry will be able to take advantage of some aspect of the advancements in HR technology.

REFERENCES

Anon. (1996), *Information Systems Management*, Section Systems Development, Winter.

Anon. (1997), *Canadian Manager*, 22 December.

Baker, E. (1997), A strategy for trimming your HR software list. *HRMagazine*, April, 37–41.

Flynn, G. (1995), HR hears the call of technology. *Personnel Journal*, **74**(5), 62–8.

Greengard, S. (1997), Leverage the power of the internet. *Workforce*, **76**(3), 76–85.

Greengard, S. (1998a), Building a self-service culture that works. *Workforce*, **77**(7), 60–4.

Greengard, S. (1998b), Putting online recruiting to work. *Workforce*, **77**(8), 73–6.

Institute of Personnel and Development in the UK (IPD) (1996) *Response to*

Home Office Consultation Paper on the EC Data Protection Directive #95/46/EC. http://www.ipd.co.uk/policy/respond.htm.

Minneman, W. A. (1996), Strategic justification for an HRIS that adds value. *HRMagazine*, **41**(12), 35–7.

Richards-Carpenter, C. (1997), *1997 Computers in Personnel and Training Survey.* Institute of Personnel and Development and the Institute for Employment Studies. http://www.employment-studies.co.uk/summary/cip97sum.html.

Samuel Greengard Workforce (1998), Making dollars and sense out of employee self-service. **77**(7), 67–9, July. At http://www.workforceonline.com/members/research/hrms/3150.html.

Sunoo, B. (1995), New directions for HRMS. *Personnel Journal*, March, Section User Friendly.

CHAPTER SEVEN

Absenteeism and Turnover in the Hospitality Industry

Abraham Pizam and Taylor Ellis

INTRODUCTION

The hospitality industry has been characterized as having excessive levels of both absenteeism and turnover. This is also true of the small to medium-sized sector. With the increasingly high cost of replacing employees, it is in the best interests of hospitality managers to understand the causes and effects of turnover and absenteeism so that they may reduce the occurrence of each. The goal of this chapter is to familiarize the reader with the most current information related to turnover and absenteeism. While it is not our intent to prescribe a series of universal steps that could lower absenteeism and turnover, we nevertheless feel that by understanding the factors that are associated with their occurrence, specific factors could be devised that may reduce their pervasiveness. Research and popular opinion hold that both turnover and absenteeism have similar effects and determinants. It is for this reason that we are discussing these two concepts together.

Absenteeism and turnover

For the purposes of this chapter, the terms absenteeism and turnover are defined as follows. Absenteeism takes place when employees do not report to work. It can take two forms: authorized or unauthorized. Under most circumstances authorized or scheduled absenteeism does not have a negative effect on a company since management can plan for the employee's absence, and the impact of this absence will be minimal or non-existent. On the other hand, unauthorized or unscheduled absences can cause substantial hardships for the company, fellow employees, and customers alike. For this reason, this chapter will concentrate on unauthorized absenteeism. Turnover can take several forms: it can be voluntary or involuntary, functional or dysfunctional, avoidable or unavoidable. Voluntary turnover occurs when employees leave a company of their own free will. Involuntary turnover is when employees are dismissed, laid off, or forced to retire (Mobley, 1982). Functional turnover occurs when poor performers leave, and dysfunctional turnover occurs when good performers leave (Dalton, Todor and Krackhardt, 1982). Unavoidable turnover occurs when an organization has absolutely no control over the reason for an employee's exit, such as for relocation to follow spouse, for pregnancy and for staying home to take care of spouse or children. Avoidable turnover occurs when employees leave a company for better pay, better working conditions, problems with superiors, etc. (Abelson, 1987). While the financial consequences of all types of turnover are similar (i.e. replacing the employee and the associated costs of advertising the position, interviewing, training, etc.), most hospitality practitioners are more interested in the reduction of voluntary, dysfunctional and avoidable turnover.

The prevalence and consequences of absenteeism

Excessive absenteeism can have a serious impact on any company, but especially on smaller ones where individual employees have more key responsibilities than their counterparts in large organizations. The seriousness of this impact is subject to extensive debate. According to a study conducted in the United States of America, 'Employee absenteeism is on the rise – increasing by 14 per cent since 1992 – and so is the cost to employers. Absenteeism costs companies an average of [US]$505 per employee in 1994, up from [US]$487 in 1993' (CCH Incorporation, 1995, p. 9). The International Personnel Management Association estimates that sick leave costs range from US$200 to almost US$650 per employee, depending on the benefits package (Boles and Sunoo, 1998). This cost figure appears to be only the tip of the iceberg. In a 1997 interview, restaurateur Carbone suggested that it costs an average of US$1500 to replace an employee, and that is not counting actual 'hard costs'. Hard costs are defined as those costs that can be directly measured as resulting from the absenteeism, such as hiring a temporary employee. Replacing a manager costs US$15000 (Walkup, 1997).

While these direct costs seem very substantial given the number of employees in the hospitality industry, the total cost is much harder to estimate and probably considerably higher. This is because direct costs do not take into consideration the following indirect costs, which are much harder to estimate:

- overtime paid to cover unscheduled absences;
- temporary help to fill in for absent employees;
- time spent rearranging work schedules;
- time spent by absentees catching up when they return;
- decreased morale and productivity of workers who have to compensate for absentees;
- lost revenue from customer dissatisfaction caused by poor service. (McKee, 1992)

When studying absenteeism Buschak and Craven (1996) found that at least 50 per cent of all employee absenteeism is not caused by *bona fide* illness or other acceptable reasons. They found that absenteeism created productivity problems, put an unfair burden on the majority of employees who showed up for work, hindered customer satisfaction, and depleted the country's economy. They estimated that in 1994 absenteeism in US firms resulted in the loss of over 400 million workdays – an average of approximately 5.1 days per employee. This translated into an annual loss of US$40 billion. In general it was found that:

- unionized firms had higher absenteeism rates than non-unionized firms;
- women were absent more than men;
- single persons were absent more than married persons. (Buschak and Craven, 1996)

These numbers, however, may not necessarily represent the hospitality industry, where absenteeism is considered to be lower than in manufacturing, and especially among blue-collar workers.

Causes of absenteeism

In their study on absenteeism, Nico and Hagedoorn (1996) found that employees' perception of inequity in the workplace was related to their intention to withdraw, which resulted in the employee calling in sick. However, even employees that perceived inequitable situations were less likely to call in sick or resign when they felt involved in their jobs. Even more interesting was the fact that employees who felt deprived and perceived an intolerant group norm regarding absenteeism were less likely to call in sick. In extreme situations, employees who perceived inequities and were under stress or tension were more likely to withdraw permanently by resigning than by withdrawing temporarily through absenteeism.

In an attempt to shed additional light on absenteeism Goodwins Brooke

& Dickenson and HRStrategies (1996) surveyed 1000 employees for the purpose of identifying the reasons employees call in sick. Their findings indicate that:

- single employees with children missed significantly more work time owing to a sick child than did married employees with children;
- women missed significantly more work than men owing to child or elder care;
- they also missed more time owing to stress and personal illness;
- employees over 50 missed significantly more work owing to personal illness;
- employees aged 30 to 39 missed more workdays owing to stress than any other age group.

The average employee with dependants missed 6.4 work days a year to take care of a child or elderly dependant or for another personal matter. The missed time increased to 11 days a year when time spent at work to handle personal matters was included.

Other researchers found that the prevalence of absenteeism was higher among organizations that had:

- poor employee morale;
- personnel conflicts;
- unsatisfactory compensation and benefit programmes;
- employees with unrealistic job expectations;
- inadequate training;
- unsafe or stressful workplace conditions. (Buschak and Craven, 1996)

Methods to reduce absenteeism

Most experts agree that the key to eliminating absenteeism is to analyse why the employee is abusing the company's sick-leave policy. One has to look for trends in sick-leave for example, and examine whether it is higher in one department or under a specific supervisor. Furthermore, careful attention should be given to workplace practices or policies affecting the use of sick leave. Determining the effects on employees' absenteeism of such factors as children's illnesses and elderly parents' disability is of critical importance. Only by finding the root of the problem can one design long-term solutions. Popular suggestions for lowering absenteeism include attendance bonus programmes, sick-leave incentives and annual recognition for minimal sick-leave use (Boles and Sunoo, 1998).

The prevalence and consequences of turnover

Voluntary employee turnover is a phenomenon of extensive interest to theorists and practitioners of Human Resource Management (HRM). HRM theorists have been fascinated by its causes and correlates, and practitioners have been interested in it because of its high costs and negative effects on the organization. According to the United States, Bureau of Labor Statistics (1996), the average turnover rate in all US industries in 1995 was 13 per cent. In comparison, the turnover rate in the hospitality industry was estimated to be much higher (Fortino and Ninemeir, 1996) and ranged from 58 to 154 per cent among staff, and 15 to 48 per cent among management personnel. In the same year, the average turnover for the hotel industry was estimated by the PKF accounting firm to be 53.2 per cent (Hotel Business, 1997).

In the hospitality industry there is some evidence to suggest that turnover varies by the size of the establishment, and, more specifically, that larger establishments have a more severe turnover problem than smaller establishments (Peacock, 1993). Possible explanations for this variation may be found in the type of establishment. Small businesses are usually not part of a larger operation such as a 'chain'. They are usually a single outlet, operated as a sole proprietorship, more likely to hire individuals they know, and more stable. A major chain or corporation will most likely use a more impersonal hiring procedure, and this will result in errors and attract employees that intend to move to other jobs in an attempt to gain experience or to further their career. However, the negative consequences of labour turnover are similar for establishments of all sizes. Also, most researchers agree that issues such as 'individual contract making' between managers and employees, and despotic styles of leadership, do little to prevent labour turnover and absenteeism in smaller establishments.

In a study conducted among managers and employees of over 160 UK hospitality companies Harbourne (1995) attempted to analyse employees' turnover intentions. The results indicated that over 25 per cent of the full-time and 30 per cent of the part-time respondents expected to leave their present jobs in the next twelve months. Even more interesting was the effect of the respondents' age on the expectation of leaving their present employment:

Looking at the figures more closely, we find that turnover is highest among younger respondents, particularly those aged 20 to 29. This group can be further subdivided. In one camp, you will find people who dip in and out of the industry on their way to careers in other sectors. Typically, these are students working in pubs and restaurants to supplement their meager grants, or people between jobs who need paid employment for a couple of months. In the other camp, there are those who intend to make a career in the industry, but who need to move on to gain experience and/or promotion. There are so many small businesses in the industry that it is unrealistic to expect a talented newcomer to stay too long in any one establishment. (Harbourne, 1995, p. 39)

Simons (1995), in a study among hotel employees, found that younger hotel employees ranked job security low on their list of items desired. This preference is manifested through their job-hopping behaviour, which is generally common, specifically for younger employees, among those working in the hospitality industry. According to Simons, most hospitality workers in the early portion of their career expect to move from job to job, which could explain the low desirability placed on job security.

As one can imagine, the tangible and intangible costs associated with turnover are exorbitant and continually increasing. As suggested by Mobley (1982), the negative consequences of turnover for the firm are:

- economic costs for separation, replacement and training;
- productivity losses;
- impaired service quality;
- lost business opportunities;
- increased administrative burden;
- demoralization of stayers.

As for economic costs, in a study conducted by Hom (1992) among mental health professionals, it was found that the total costs for separation, replacement and training for a single incidence of turnover in the position of clinician/counsellor II were US$25,681.64 as follows:

	US$
Separation costs	10,186.27

- exit interviews;
- administrative costs;
- unused vacation time;
- lost client revenues;
- overtime pay;
- temporary employment;
- case transfer to others.

Replacement costs   1,380.30
- advertisements;
- personnel recruitment;
- application processing;
- entrance interviews;
- application selection;
- miscellaneous costs (tests, travel, relocation reimbursements).

Training costs   4,115.07
- formal orientation;
- formal job training;
- off-site training;
- on-the-job training;
- client revenue loss.

Other negative consequences of turnover cannot always be easily quantified. They are nevertheless of crucial importance, as demonstrated below:

Productivity losses
- leavers often miss work or are tardy before they depart (Rosse, 1988);
- missing employees produce nothing (Rhodes and Steers, 1990);
- new replacements are less productive than veteran employees (Price, 1977);
- remaining employees' work is interrupted because they have to train the new replacement (Louis, Posner and Powell, 1983);
- impaired quality of service;
- understaffed organizations delay or withhold service (Darmon, 1990);
- new employees provide less competent and less personalized service because they don't know the customers (Darmon, 1990);
- customers may switch firms if their loyalties depend on an affinity with former sales employees (Schlesinger and Heskett, 1991);
- disgruntled employees may provide poor service before they leave (Schneider and Bowen, 1992).

Lost business opportunities
- the introduction of new products or services are delayed or prevented (Gomez-Mejia, Balkin and Milkovich, 1990);
- expatriates from existing firms may form competing businesses (Mandel and Farrell, 1992).

Increased administrative burden
- expansion of administrative staff needed to handle the extra recruiting and training (Price, 1989).

Employee demoralization
- existing employees lose friends (O'Reilly, Caldwell and Barnett, 1989);
- awareness that a leaver has found a better job may change the stayers' perception of their job (Hulin, Roznowski and Hachiya, 1985);
- the social integration of stayers is undermined, and this in turn stimulates more turnover (Price, 1989).

In the restaurant industry, turnover costs are not significantly less expensive. According to the National Restaurant Association, 'turnover costs for restaurants average about US$5000 per employee. Turnover costs for managers can average US$50,000 or more' (Woods, 1997, p. 361). At present there are no comprehensive studies to determine the magnitude of the costs of turnover in the hotel industry. Numerous comments have been made by industry executives in public fora, and this suggests that the costs of turnover are of significant proportion. The Marriott Corporation alone estimated that each one per cent increase in its employee turnover rate costs the company US$5–15 million in lost revenues (Schlesinger and Heskett, 1991).

Causes of turnover: general

It is estimated that more than 2500 studies of antecedents and correlates of turnover have been conducted to date (Woods, 1997). Unfortunately, many of these have conflicting results and few were conducted in the hospitality industry. Therefore, theoreticians and practitioners both inside and outside the hospitality industry face an increasingly bewildering flood of new and often contradictory scientific studies on every aspect of employee turnover. This has at times done more to stir up controversy than to establish reliable knowledge. Fortunately, a few researchers have managed to sort through these numberless studies and compare them in a comprehensive and systematic manner through the use of a statistical technique called meta-analysis. By numerically combining diverse research findings on a single question – such as the effect of job satisfaction on turnover – meta-analysis has been used to identify the central tendency and reach conclusions far more reliable than those of any single investigation.

Hom and Griffeth (1995) have conducted the most inclusive and comprehensive of these meta-analyses. The remaining part of this section will report their findings as they relate to: 1. demographic and personal characteristics; 2. overall job satisfaction; 3. organization and work environment; 4. job contents and intrinsic motivation; 5. external environment; 6. variables of the withdrawal process; 7. absenteeism, lateness and job performance.

The paragraphs below show the conclusions that each meta-analytical procedure made when examining the relationship between each of the seven categories and turnover.

1. Demographic and personal characteristics

- women tended to be more loyal than men and had a lower quitting rate;
- those with greater family obligations (for example, married, had more children, and had younger children) had lower quitting rates;
- older employees with long tenure had lower quitting rates than younger and short-tenure employees.

2. Overall job satisfaction

- dissatisfied employees more readily quit their jobs than satisfied employees;
- the correlation between job dissatisfaction and resignation are stronger during periods of low unemployment but weaker during periods of joblessness;
- employees whose pre-employment expectations about their jobs were *not* met, quit their jobs more readily than those whose expectations *were* met.

3. Organization and work environment

- dissatisfaction with pay (not including fringe benefits) was not associated with turnover;
- perceived fairness of levels of compensation (equity of rewards) had a very weak correlation with turnover;
- leader–member exchange (a general construct representing the interdependence between superiors and subordinates) predicted turnover more accurately than participative management, satisfaction with supervision, and leaders' communication skills;
- good peer-group relations (group cohesion) and satisfaction with co-workers decreased turnover;
- clear perception about one's role in the organization lowered turnover, whereas role overload and role conflict increased it;

- centralization of the organization (degree of power concentration in the upper echelons) and supportiveness barely affected turnover;
- satisfaction about promotions modestly predicted turnover;
- perceived opportunities for promotions modestly predicted turnover;
- actual promotions strongly predicted turnover.

4. Job contents and intrinsic motivation

- individuals for whom job complexity and the challenge of their work duties were high had lower rates of turnover than their counterparts;
- employees doing routine work were likely to quit;
- work satisfaction (experienced positive affect towards the entire intrinsic attributes of the job) exhibited a weak relationship to quitting rates;
- job stress moderately predicted turnover;
- internal or intrinsic motivation decreases turnover;
- employees who feel involved in their jobs tend to have a lower turnover rate than those who do not feel involved in their jobs;
- professionalism (adherence to professional values and norms) did not affect withdrawal rates;
- individuals who possessed a drive to manage (i.e. had managerial motivation) were less likely to quit than those who did not possess such motivation.

5. External environment

- perceived attraction and availability of other jobs only moderately encourages individuals to quit.

6. Variables of the withdrawal process

- intentions to seek alternatives or to quit best predicted actual departure;
- employees would leave their workplace if they believed that quitting would be beneficial and could avoid or minimize negative repercussions.

7. Absenteeism, lateness and job performance

- absenteeism was found to be strongly related to turnover;
- lateness was found to be correlated to turnover;
- poor performers had a moderately higher tendency to quit than good performers (Hom and Griffeth, 1995, pp. 35–49).

CAUSES OF TURNOVER: THE HOSPITALITY INDUSTRY

In the opinions of many practitioners and some researchers, including Bell and Winters (1993), much turnover in the hospitality industry is due to the fact that entry-level employees can move elsewhere easily to an employer who can provide them with better working conditions. The problem with this situation, from both the customer's and the manager's perspective, is that these are the employees that represent the company to the guest. If these employees are dissatisfied with their work situation and are willing to move for higher wages, it is probable that the level of service provided by them is also unsatisfactory. According to these researchers it should be in the manager's best interest to ensure that front-line employees are happy and provide exceptional guest service. After all, the reservationists, bell staff, front-desk clerks, and wait staff *are* the company to the guest and, as such, determine whether or not the guest has a satisfying experience.

Iverson and Deery (1997) consider that an important predictor of an individual's decision to leave a hospitality organization is that of 'turnover culture'. These authors define 'turnover culture' as the acceptance of turnover as part of the work-group norm. That is, it is a normative belief held by employees that turnover behaviour is quite appropriate. Iverson and Deery identified several variables that contributed to turnover culture. The variables that seemed to have the most impact on turnover culture were termed *structural*, *pre-entry*, *environmental*, *union* and *employee* orientations, and were defined as follows:

- *structural* variables relate to the work setting (in the sense of both organizational and job-related factors) and have an indirect impact on intention to leave via job satisfaction. Variables include co-worker and supervisory support, routinization, and distributive justice. Other structural variables comprise the four job stress factors of role ambiguity, role conflict, work overload and resource inadequacy. Pay is also expected to have a positive impact on job satisfaction, while there is strong support in the literature for the three internal labour-market elements of job security, promotional opportunity and career development;
- *pre-entry* variables comprise the positive personality traits e.g. predisposition to be generally happy; and negative personality traits e.g. predisposition to experience discomfort. These are hypothesized to have a positive and negative effect, respectively, on job satisfaction;
- *environmental* variables relate to the non-work-setting factors. These

concern job opportunity, which has been found to have a negative effect on job satisfaction and a positive effect on intent to leave. Although there is little quantitative evidence to support turnover culture, it is implied in the hospitality industry literature. Similarly, kinship responsibility is anticipated to have a direct negative impact on intent to leave;

- *union* variables, concerning whether employees are union members, have been found to be a significant predictor of both job satisfaction and turnover. In addition, there is evidence affirming the negative effect of union loyalty on intent to leave;
- *employee* orientations deal with affective responses, such as job satisfaction, organizational commitment and job search, which are produced by the structural, pre-entry, environmental and union variables. In terms of the causal ordering it is hypothesized that the second intervening variable (organizational commitment) is a function of job satisfaction, while organizational commitment is then hypothesized to have a negative impact on job search. Finally, job search behaviour is expected to be the immediate precursor of intent to leave.

Methods to reduce turnover: general

The trade and managerial literature is full of popular prescriptions for reducing turnover. Such prescriptions include:

- increasing pay and fringe benefits;
- providing child care;
- providing better career opportunities;
- improving selection of employees;
- improving orientation programmes;
- improving the quality of communication between employees and management;
- providing better definitions of the job.

While these methods are simple and sensible, Hom and Griffeth (1995) consider them to be mostly based on precarious empirical research, or derived from case studies and anecdotal evidence. Rigorous research is very scarce, especially in the form of studies using experimental or quasi-experimental design to determine the effectiveness of these and other methods of turnover reduction. Currently, there are only a handful of intervention strategies based on rigorous empirical research that have been proven to significantly reduce turnover. Among these are realistic job previews, job enrichment, workspace characteristics, socialization practices, and employee selection.

Realistic job previews

Realistic job previews (RJP) entail simply informing a prospective or new employee realistic facts about his or her job, and have been proven to reduce early attrition in some occupations such as nursing, accountancy and miscellaneous service jobs (Rynes, 1990; Wanous, 1992). RJP work best with new employees who hold naïve and inflated expectations about their new jobs and are later shocked to learn that their jobs did not meet their expectations. Such a case could be made for many tourism and hospitality employees who have glamorous expectations about their jobs. Many first-time applicants for hotel, airline, or travel agency jobs expect to rub shoulders with the 'rich and famous', travel free around the world, stay complimentarily in the best hotels, and eat gourmet cuisine at the employer's expense. Upon starting to work, these employees become disappointed when they have to work long hours and holidays, stand constantly on their feet and deal with awkward customers.

Job enrichment

Field experiments and correlational studies found that job enrichment reduced turnover even more effectively than RJP (Griffeth, 1985; McEvoy and Cascio, 1985). As it turned out, those employees who used a variety of skills, completed an identifiable piece of work, performed tasks that had some significance to others, had some autonomy in performing their job and received feedback on their job performance – all characteristics of enriched jobs – had lower turnover rates.

Workspace characteristics

In a series of studies, Oldham (Oldham and Rotchform, 1983; Oldham and Fried, 1987; Oldham, 1988; Oldham, Kulik and Stepina, 1991) found that workspace attributes affected morale, dissatisfaction, work avoidance and turnover. High worker density, dim lighting, drab wall colours and few enclosures (numerous employees working in one large space) explained 24 per cent of office employees' turnover.

Socialization practices

Evidence accumulated over many years suggests that, as a group, new employees have a much higher turnover rate than veteran employees. This may be a significant factor in smaller establishments because many employees are seasonal and have little chance of becoming veterans unless they are employed on a year-round basis. Researchers (Fisher, 1986; Feldman, 1988) suggest that this excessive turnover rate is caused by inadequate or incomplete organizational socialization. Among the socialization programmes that were found to be effective in reducing turnover were:

- off-site residential training and business trips among business graduates (Louis, Posner and Powell, 1983);
- reality shock (a long-term comprehensive orientation programme that consists of lectures, rap-sessions, conflict resolution workshops) among nurses (Weiss, 1984);
- self-management training (programmes designed to assist newcomers in developing mechanisms for coping with transition stress and improving job survival) (Manz and Sims, 1989).

Employee selection

At present, several employee characteristics that can be detected during the selection process have been found to be moderate predictors of turnover. Among these are:

- biographical data (i.e. employee referrals, prior experience, educational attainment) (Breaugh and Dossett, 1989);
- personality characteristics such as negative affectivity (a trait signifying a constantly experienced negative emotional state) (George, 1990); poor person–organization fit (Chatman, 1991); conscientiousness; openness to experience; agreeableness (Barrick and Mount, 1991).

Methods to reduce turnover: the hospitality industry

Empirical research related to methods of curbing turnover in the small to medium-sized sector of the hospitality industry is extremely scarce and none of it has been done in a quasi-experimental or field-experimental method. Nonetheless, a few studies that have been conducted shed an important light on this topic. These studies suggest that turnover rates can be reduced by:

- provision of job security via long-term contracts (Simms, Hales and Riley, 1988);
- strategically placed induction programmes highlighting the organization's aim for long-term employment (Denvir and McMahon, 1992);
- provision of selected benefits (e.g. retirement plans, group vision insurance, group dental insurance, group life insurance). However, other benefits, such as child care, transportation and numerous miscellaneous fringe benefits, did not have any effect on turnover (Ohlin and West, 1993);
- availability of internal labour markets ('hire-from-within' policy), since these promote employee commitment (Woods and Macauley, 1989; Debrah, 1994);
- availability of supervisory and management career-path programmes (Woods and Macauley, 1989);
- union loyalty – employees' commitment to a local union (Deery, Iverson and Erwin, 1994; Iverson and Deery, 1997);
- hiring of older employees (Harbourne, 1995).

Iverson and Deery (1997) summarize the findings of their study along with the research of others and conclude that the hospitality industry tends to create and reinforce a turnover culture. Employees enter believing their careers will be limited. This position may be countered by establishing promotion from within organizations and by encouraging union membership among workers. Deery and Iverson continue by proposing that a variety of recruitment and selection methods should be used, including a formal referral system; the hiring of minorities, the elderly and the disabled; more rigorous interviewing procedures; realistic job previews; bio-data collection; and personality tests.

Comprehensive models

In the past two decades, several authors have proposed numerous comprehensive models that attempt to explain the correlates of both absenteeism and turnover. Though the majority of these models do not specifically relate to the hospitality industry or services in general, the models presented by Schlesinger and Heskett (1991) and by Pizam (1982) have addressed these issues within both these contexts.

As can be seen from Figure 7.1 (p. 124), Schlesinger and Heskett propose that poor wages, lack of career opportunities, insufficient training, simple and repetitive tasks, and lack of control over one's job, cause dissatisfaction

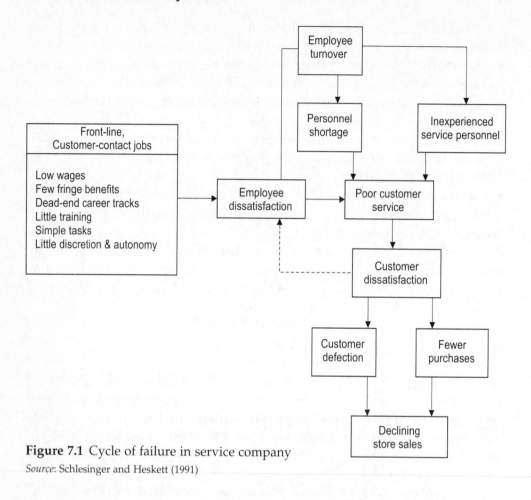

Figure 7.1 Cycle of failure in service company
Source: Schlesinger and Heskett (1991)

among front-line, customer-contact employees. This job-dissatisfaction leads to poor customer service, which in turn leads to constantly protesting and dissatisfied customers. The negative feelings of the customers create irritation and frustration among employees who become even more dissatisfied with their jobs and end up leaving the organization. Though at present the empirical studies that were conducted on this topic cannot fully confirm this model, most practitioners and researchers would speculate that it may be a good partial representation of the turnover and absenteeism phenomenon in many service organizations, including hospitality and tourism services. While Schlesinger and Heskett suggest that turnover, and possibly absenteeism, in service firms are caused by the characteristics of one's job and the organizational reward system, Pizam's model alleges that absenteeism and turnover in hospitality enterprises are caused by a combination of characteristics, some of which are internal to the organization and others of which are external to it. As can be seen from Figure 7.2, western societies have attached a stigma to many hospitality front-line jobs. Therefore, these jobs create feelings of inferiority among their incumbents and tend to attract a disproportionate number of foreigners or minorities. This in turn re-inforces the negative images of these jobs and discourages good potential employees.

The characteristics of the hospitality industry are such that they create an unpleasant work environment. Symptomatic of the industry as a whole, and reflective of the nature of the business, are such conditions as seasonality of operation, prevalence of small firms, unpleasant physical work-conditions, inconvenient patterns of working hours, lack of career opportunities for many front-line jobs, and even low pay. Therefore, the characteristics of society, coupled with those of the industry, lead to high rates of job dissatisfaction, absenteeism and turnover among front-line hospitality employees.

SUMMARY AND CONCLUSIONS

As can be seen from the preceding discussion, the causes of both turnover and absenteeism are complex. Owing to this complexity, there is no one, single, easy fix. It is up to the hospitality manager to determine the possible contributors to each individual situation. Once the possible causes have been determined, the appropriate action can be taken. It is important to note that there are no prescribed formulae or guide-lines that will work in every situation. Rather, hospitality managers must attempt to analyse the situation and, using their analysis, determine an appropriate course of action.

It is important to keep in mind that the best solution for turnover may take place before the employee is even hired. Selection procedures and characteristics of the employee have been shown to affect both turnover and absenteeism. Therefore, managers should determine the characteristics that they are seeking *prior* to the selection process, and hire only those individuals that meet the criteria. The issues of turnover and absenteeism are major factors in every business and require considerable managerial time. However, if the dual problems of turnover and absenteeism can be reduced, there will be a significant, positive impact on the company.

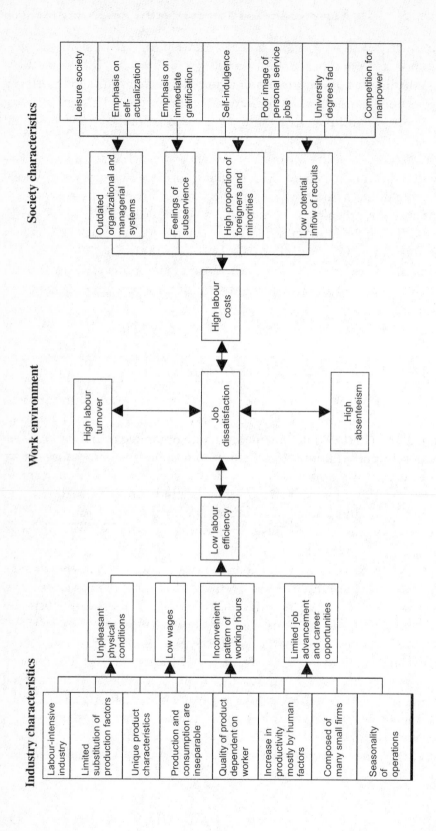

Figure 7.2 Tourism's work environment and its determinants

Source: Pizam (1982)

REFERENCES

Abelson, M. A. (1987), Examination of avoidable and unavoidable turnover. *Journal of Applied Psychology*, **72**, 382–6.

Barrick, M. R. and Mount, M. K. (1991), The big five personality dimensions and job performance: a meta-analysis. *Personnel Psychology*, **44**, 1–26.

Bell, R. A. and Winters, L. C. (1993), Using marketing tools to improve employee relations. *Cornell Hotel and Restaurant Administration Quarterly*, **34**(6), 38–42.

Boles, M. and Sunoo, P. B. (1998), Remedy sick leave abuse. *Workforce*, **77**(1), 22.

Breaugh, J. A. and Dossett, D. L. (1989), Rethinking the use of personal history information: the value of theory-based biodata for predicting turnover. *Journal of Business and Psychology*, **3**, 371–85.

Buschak, M. and Craven, C. (1996), Managing absenteeism for greater productivity. *Advanced Management Journal*, **61**(1), 26–31.

CCH Incorporation (1995), Curbing absenteeism. *HR Focus*, **72**(12), 9.

Chatman, J. A. (1991), Matching people and organizations: selection and socialization in public accounting firms. *Administrative Science Quarterly*, **36**, 459–84.

Dalton, D. R., Todor, W. D. and Krackhardt, D. M. (1982), Turnover overstated: a functional taxonomy. *Academy of Management Review*, **7**, 117–23.

Darmon, R. Y. (1990), Identifying sources of turnover costs: a segmental approach. *Journal of Marketing*, **54**, 46–56.

Debrah, Y. A. (1994), Management of operative staff in a labour-scarce economy: the views of human resource managers in the hotel industry in Singapore. *Asia Pacific Journal of Human Resources*, **32**(1), 1–60.

Deery, S. J., Iverson, R. D. and Erwin, P. J. (1994), Predicting organizational and union commitment: the effect of industrial relations climate. *British Journal of Industrial Relations*, **32**(4), 581–97.

Denvir, A. and McMahon, F. (1992), Labour turnover in London hotels and the cost effectiveness of preventative measures. *International Journal of Hospitality Management*, **11**(2), 143–54.

Feldman, D. C. (1988), *Managing Careers in Organizations*. Glenview, IL: Scott, Foresman.

Fisher, C. D. (1986), Organizational socialization: an integrative review. In K. Rowland and G. Ferris (eds), *Research in Personnel and Human Resources Management*, vol. 4. Greenwich, CT: JAI Press, pp. 101–46.

Fortino, P. and Ninemeir, J. (1996), Industry in the dark about turnover rate. *Lodging*, December, p. 25.

George, J. M. (1990), Personality, affect, and behavior in groups. *Journal of Applied Psychology*, **75**, 107–16.

Goodwins, Brooke & Dickenson and HRStrategies (1996), Who misses work, and why? *HR Focus*, **73**, 3.

Gomez-Mejia, L. R., Balkin, D. B. and Milkovich, G. T. (1990), Rethinking your rewards for technical employees. *Organizational Dynamics*, **18**, 62–75.

Griffeth, R. W. (1985), Moderation of the effects of job enrichment by participation: a longitudinal field experiment. *Organizational Behavior and Human Decision Processes*, **35**, 73–93.

Harbourne, D. (1995), Issues in hospitality and catering. *Management Development Review*, **8**(1), 37–40.

Hom, P. (1992), *Turnover Costs Among Mental Health Professionals*. New York: Van Nostrand Reinhold.

Hom, P. W. and Griffeth, R. W. (1995), *Employee Turnover*. South-Western College, Ohio.

Hotel Business (1997), Turnover. 21 December 1996 – 7 January 1997, p. 3.

Hulin, C. L., Roznowski, M. and Hachiya, D. (1985), Alternative opportunities and withdrawal decisions: empirical and theoretical discrepancies and an integration. *Psychological Bulletin*, **97**, 233–50.

Iverson, R. D. and Deery, M. (1997), Turnover culture in the hospitality industry. *Human Resource Management Journal*, **7**(4), 71–82.

Louis, M. R., Posner, B. Z. and Powell, G. N. (1983), The availability and helpfulness of socialization practices. *Personnel Psychology*, **36**, 857–66.

Mandel, M. J. and Farrell, C. (1992), The immigrants. *Business Week*, 13 July, p. 114.

Manz, C. C. and Sims, H. P. (1989), *Super Leadership*. New York: John Wiley.

McEvoy, G. M. and Cascio, W. F. (1985), Strategies for reducing employee turnover: a meta-analysis. *Journal of Applied Psychology*, **70**, 342–53.

McKee, B. (1992), The hidden costs of absenteeism. *Nation's Business*, **80**(6), 10–12.

Mobley, W. H. (1982), *Employee Turnover: Causes, Consequences, and Control*, Reading, MA: Addison Wesley.

Nico, W. V. Y. and Hagedoorn, M. (1996), Intent to leave and absenteeism as reactions to perceived inequity: the role of psychological and social constraints. *Journal of Occupational and Organizational Psychology*, **69**(4), 367–8.

Ohlin, J. B. and West, J. J. (1993), An analysis of the fringe benefit offerings on the turnover of hourly housekeeping workers in the hotel industry. *International Journal of Hospitality Management*, **12**(4), 323–36.

Oldham, G. R. (1988), Effects of change in workspace partitions and spatial density on employee reactions: a quasi-experiment. *Journal of Applied Psychology*, **73**, 253–8.

Oldham, G. R. and Fried, Y. (1987), Employee reactions to workspace characteristics. *Journal of Applied Psychology*, **72**, 75–80.

Oldham, G. R. and Rotchform, N. L. (1983), Relationships between office characteristics and employee reactions: a study of the physical environment. *Administrative Science Quarterly*, **28**, 542–56.

Oldham, G. R., Kulik, C. T. and Stepina, L. P. (1991), Physical environments and employee reactions: effects of stimulus-screening skills and job complexity. *Academy of Management Journal*, **34**(4), 929–38.

O'Reilly, C. A., Caldwell, D. F. and Barnett, W. P. (1989), Work group demography, social integration, and turnover. *Administrative Science Quarterly*, **34**, 21–37.

Peacock, M. (1993), A question of size. *International Journal of Contemporary Hospitality Management*, **5**(4), 29–32.

Pizam, A. (1982), Tourism manpower: the state of the art. *Journal of Travel Research*, **21**(2), 5–9.

Price, J. L. (1977), *The Study of Turnover*. Ames, IA: Iowa State University Press.

Price, J. L. (1989), The impact of turnover on the organization. *Work and Occupations*, **16**, 461–73.

Rhodes, S. R. and Steers, R. M. (1990), *Managing Employee Absenteeism*. Reading, MA: Addison-Wesley.

Rosse, J. G. (1988), Relations among lateness, absence, and turnover: is there a progression of withdrawal? *Human Relations*, **41**, 517–31.

Rynes, S. L. (1990), Recruitment, job choice, and post-hire consequences: a call for new research directions. In M. D. Dunnette and L. Hough (eds), *Handbook of Industrial and Organizational Psychology*, 2nd edn. Palo Alto, CA: Consulting Psychologists Press, pp. 399–444.

Schlesinger, L. A. and Heskett, J. L. (1991), The service-driven service company. *Harvard Business Review*, **69**, 71–81.

Schneider, B. and Bowen, D. (1992), Personnel/human resources management in the service sector. In G. Ferris and K. Rowland (eds), *Research in Personnel and Human Resources Management*. Greenwich, CT: JAI Press, chapter 10, pp. 1–30.

Simms, J., Hales, C. and Riley, M. (1988), Examination of the concept of the internal labour markets in UK hotels. *Tourism Management*, 3–12 March.

Simons, T. (1995), Motivating hotel employees. *Cornell Hotel and Restaurant Administration Quarterly*, **36**(1), 20–7.

United States, Bureau of Labor Statistics (1996), *Bureau of Labor Statistics for Business*. Washington, DC: US Department of Labor.

Walkup, C. (1997), Build a positive culture by including personal values. *Nation's Restaurant News*, **31**(23), p. 70.

Wanous, J. P. (1992), *Organizational Entry*, 2nd edn. New York: Addison-Wesley.

Weiss, S. J. (1984), The effect of transition modules on new graduate adaption. *Research in Nursing and Health*, **7**, 51–9.

Woods, R. H. (1997), *Managing Hospitality Human Resources*, 2nd edn. Lansing, MI: American Hotel & Motel Association.

Woods, R. and Macauley, J. (1989), Human resources: Rx for turnover: retention programs that work: long the bane of the hospitality industry, turnover has become even more troublesome today. *Cornell Hotel and Restaurant Administration Quarterly*, **30**(1), 78–90.

PART THREE

Operations:
Best Practice

CHAPTER EIGHT

Inheriting Staff: Managing Change and Building a Team

Amanda Lee-Ross

INTRODUCTION

Two of the most frequent and challenging roles for managers are managing change and team-building. At some point in a manager's life, there will be change to implement and new staff to deal with. This may be due to organizational change, recruitment, internal promotion, or even the decision to start up one's own business. As a new manager, possibly promoted from within an organization, you will be expected to work with and manage a group of people of which you were perhaps once part. If your position has been achieved by moving to a different organization or by acquiring a business, it is likely that you will be taking over staff previously managed by someone else. It may also be the case that as the new proprietor of a business you may need to make some organizational changes such as 'down-sizing' or the alteration of staff roles and responsibilities. Managing change of this kind is stressful for both employees and managers, and can make team-building difficult. Hospitality small to medium-sized enterprises (SMEs) have fewer staff, and managers often work alongside employees in operational roles. There is therefore less of a 'buffer' between staff and owner/managers than in large organizations. Tensions arising from any changes made will be felt immediately by both managers and staff.

Many generic human resource management (HRM) texts contain change-management and team-building theories but are oriented towards larger enterprises. Their applicability to SMEs such as public houses is therefore questionable. In addition, HRM texts concerning hospitality concentrate on large enterprises, and almost exclusively on hotels and catering. The public house sector is usually amalgamated with large chain operations such as Harvester Restaurants. This seems inappropriate when the majority of the hospitality sector is made up of SMEs, a fact which Roberts highlights:

> Examples are provided throughout this text of current personnel and HRM practice, the majority of which are from medium to large size hospitality companies or businesses. The industry, however, is predominated by small catering businesses – the thousands of pubs, clubs, cafés, restaurants, bed and breakfast establishments, guest houses and takeaways which make up the hospitality industry. For the small business, often operated by an owner manager, a significant part of this text may appear inappropriate. (1995, p. 3)

Small to medium-sized enterprises are ignored because, for organizations with only a few workers, many elements of employment legislation are deemed irrelevant. However, while employment legislation impacts differently on SMEs, this should not detract from the essential role employees play when servicing customers. Managers need to be able to implement change and organize their staff irrespective of organizational size.

Courses and books specifically designed for owner/managers taking over public houses deal with practical aspects of running a pub such as beer handling, value added tax (VAT) and pay as you earn (PAYE) returns, customer relations, marketing, catering, and profit calculation. Surprisingly they fail to cover the critical areas of change management or team-building, and consistently fail to address human resource issues apart from some of the negative aspects such as 'fiddling' (for example, see Wright, 1984; Stevenson, 1986). This appears to reflect the negative view of staff some owner/managers hold. Because of the lack of formal HRM training, these owner/managers may be prone to making 'snap' decisions when it comes to firing 'unsuitable' staff. In some cases this may be justified. All managers should be vigilant because staff theft (or 'fiddling' as it is often called) may have a significant impact on the business. However, this negative attitude also tends to be the policy when encountering untrained or poorly trained staff, particularly when new owners take over a business. Rather than retrain staff Wright advises that:

> it is easier to change most of the part-time bar staff when you take over, so that you can train new ones, institute your own house rules, and present a united image to the customers. We were fortunate to acquire one evening barmaid . . . who fitted in well with us. But this will not often occur . . . (1984, p. 27)

While there can be a down side to inheriting staff, it is my experience that workers have a number of good points which may prove useful to new managers. These are summarized in Table 8.1. Rather than making signifi-

Table 8.1 Inherited staff: good and bad points

Good points	Bad points
• Know the business – possibly better than the new manager or owner at first	• Know the business – possibly able to 'fiddle'
• Trained	• Training may not be to your standards
• Know the clientele – good customer relations, customers perceive continuity	• Loyalty may lie with ex-manager or owner
• Relief at being 'kept on' may lead to improved customer service as staff seek to 'prove' themselves to the new manager	• Realization of the insecurity of employment brought about by the change of manager or owner may lead to demotivation and decrease in customer service

cant changes to the business's organization, for example, by sacking staff (especially if this is not required on economic grounds), it is preferable to identify positive issues and build a successful team of workers. This chapter focuses on practical steps necessary to manage change and build teams within an SME. Initially, definitions of the public house sector and SMEs are provided, before some of the major change-management and team-building theories are discussed in the context of SMEs. In conclusion, practical recommendations are made for change management and team-building within SMEs.

The public house sector and SMEs

There is a paucity of well-defined information about the UK public house sector. In many instances it is included in categories relating to accommodation and catering. For example, Blunt (1995, p. 89) uses the term 'pubs' to include establishments with ten or more guest bedrooms, while Labour Market Data (1998) uses the category 'public houses and bars' (SIC [UK Standard Industrial Classification]: 55.4, 1989), which may include bars within hotels and restaurants. In preference to relying on ill-defined definitions (and thus inaccurate quotas) a private communication with the author of this chapter (Hampson, 1998) revealed that in 1997 there were just over 61,000 public houses in Britain. In this instance, 'public house' (or 'pub') refers to an establishment with a full on-licence that predominantly sells beer.[1] Of the 61,000 pubs, the vast majority

(27,700) are tenancies or leased pubs[2] and can effectively be classed as SMEs.

Figures collected by Labour Market Data (1988) show that 210,500 people were employed in the category 'public houses and bars' (SIC: 663, 1980), with this figure rising over the past ten years to nearly 388,000 in 1998. Seventy per cent of those employed work part time and of these, women make up 72 per cent (200,000) of all part-time workers. However, the numbers employed in public houses may be underestimated because, with the prevalence of part-time working (over 275,000 employees work part time), wage levels tend to be low. In some cases it can be difficult to attract staff, especially those in receipt of government benefits that may have to be surrendered or reduced on securing any form of employment. To help cover this 'recruitment gap' some managers may be tempted to flout official rules and not record all employees through the business books (see Mars and Nicod, 1984; Lee-Ross, 1996).

Small to medium-sized enterprises make up the majority of organizations in the UK hospitality sector. However, as with pubs, there are varying definitions (often based on employee numbers) of what an SME is. For example, Purcell and Quinn (1995) describe a small enterprise as a maximum of 99 employees; Radiven and Lucas (1996) consider organizations employing 25 or fewer employees to be small businesses. Both are reasonable, but for the purposes of this chapter, SMEs are defined as businesses that employ 50 or fewer people (with 0–25 employees being a small enterprise and 26–50 relating to medium-sized businesses).

Change-management theories

Change is inevitable in all organizations and occurs for many reasons, for example, to replenish lost skills when people leave; to implement new production techniques; to increase profits; and to increase market share. However, introducing change can be problematic as it often encounters resistance. The new goals and benefits may not be clear to staff, and they may perceive a risk to their job security. In some cases people will resist change because it upsets their normal work practices. When taking over a small business, the change process is usually much quicker and more noticeable than that in larger organizations. Large mergers and acquisitions are usually the subject of speculation and debate (within the company and sometimes in the media) for several months before the transition takes place. Therefore, staff and management have longer to become familiar with their new situation. Change in SMEs, on the other hand, happens as a reaction to a specific 'trigger'. This could be the selling or acquisition of a business, an integral member of staff leaving unexpectedly, or a new business opening in close proximity and creating greater market competition. As well as having to manage organizational change, managers also undergo a similar transition during their own careers. For example, a newly appointed manager must be able to manage his or her change in status (perhaps the shift from team member to team's leader). A corollary of this is the need for organizational change: the team has to be restructured because of the manager's promotion. It can also be argued that within small organizations, change affects more people. For instance, if a business operates with ten employees, the sacking of one member of staff will be felt significantly throughout the organization, both structurally and personally. Being able to manage change (both organizational and personal), therefore, is an integral part of a manager's role, especially in SMEs.

Change-management theories usually mention the value of 'participative' management and 'top-down' approaches. Participative management is where a manager develops an understanding of, and sensitivity to, the needs of workers. This is expressed by a willingness to listen to what employees have to say (in terms of both criticisms and suggestions for improvement), and a willingness either to act on these or to explain why it is impossible or impractical to do so. Commitment may also be gained by making subordinates' jobs more interesting, demanding or satisfying (Lupton, 1986). Top-down management follows hierarchical lines and assumes that those at the top are more competent, accountable and responsible than those at the bottom. The combination of competence and responsibility confers upon management its right to manage. This is what Lupton (1986, p. 56) calls 'managerial prerogative', and he cites McGregor, Blake and Likert as examples of theorists who believe that if change is to take place it needs to be participative but implemented in a top-down fashion. However, Lupton (1986, p. 58) disagrees with this position, arguing that being a manager 'does not automatically confer wisdom greater than that found amongst people who are not, and are never likely to become, managers'. He also argues that, because of managerial prerogative, participation never really happens, i.e. the control of change stays at the top. He argues instead for 'bottom-up' change management. This involves setting up a project team to gain an understanding of how the business runs and to diagnose the problems. The team should, however, be skilled in management and include 'well-trained, ambitious people . . . drawn from specialist activities' (1986, p. 64).

Fast   **Slower**

Clearly planned	Not clearly planned at beginning
Little involvement of others	Lots of involvement of others
Attempt to overcome any resistance: coercion	Attempt to minimize resistance: participation

Figure 8.1 Strategic continuum

Adapted from: Kotter and Schlesinger (1986)

Kotter (1995) has developed an eight-step model to instigate organizational change:

- establish a sense of urgency for the change;
- form a powerful guiding coalition, i.e. assemble a group with enough power to lead the change;
- create a vision;
- communicate the vision. Use every possible means of communicating the new vision including using the behaviour of the guiding coalition;
- empower others to act on the vision, i.e. encourage risk-taking and non-traditional ideas;
- plan for and create short-term wins;
- consolidate the improvements, i.e. hire, promote and develop employees who can implement the vision;
- institutionalize the new approaches.

According to Kotter and Schlesinger (1986), the speed with which change should be implemented depends on many factors. These include the amount and type of resistance anticipated; the presence or lack of a crisis; the consequences of lack of change; the availability or unavailability of information with which to make a decision; and the power of the change agent. They argue that there is a strategic continuum for the speed of change, and such a model is shown in Figure 8.1. At one end of the continuum the strategy would call for a slower change process, with greater involvement of employees. At the other end, the change strategy needs to be implemented swiftly, with little involvement of others. However, Kotter and Schlesinger argue that managers often 'move too quickly and involve too few people despite the fact that they do not have all the information they really need to design the change correctly' (1986, p. 170).

Pugh (1986, pp. 143–5) has six rules for managing change effectively. These are:

- work hard at establishing the need for change. For change to be effective there needs to be a reason that is acceptable to interest groups and those involved in the change (e.g. changing customer demand);
- think through the change, i.e. be aware of what the change will mean to others. In this way, the manager can identify potential points of resistance;
- initiate change through informal discussion to get feedback and participation;
- encourage those concerned to give their objections. By encouraging contributions, people are less likely to rigidly oppose the change;
- be prepared to change yourself. Do not fall in love with your own idea and be prepared to accept that change may be 'bottom-up';
- monitor the change and reinforce it.

For managers of SMEs, particularly in the hospitality sector, there are problems with Lupton's, Kotter's and Pugh's change models. This is because of the smaller numbers of employees; the management style; the speed of change needed; and the nature of employment and career prospects within hospitality SMEs.

Number of employees

The models of Lupton and Kotter assume that the organization has enough employees to be able either to set up a project team (Lupton) or to form a strong group that identifies with the change in order to push it through (Kotter). In a small business, with fewer employees than large organizations, there tend to be less departmentalism and bureaucracy, and fewer management layers. Quite often there is a management hierarchy of only one or two people. For instance, in a public house this could be a bar manager and the owner/manager. It could, therefore, be difficult to form a coalition to push change through. A positive aspect for SMEs, however, is that fewer management layers and staff, and less bureaucracy, likely to cause less resistance to change. This is because it is unlikely for a strong group to form that can resist the change.

Management style

Management style is simply the range of behaviours that managers can use to deal with people and work situations. There are four main management styles, which can be described as *autocratic*, *paternalistic*, *consultative*, and *team oriented*. These range from autocratic at one extreme to team oriented at the other. Management style is influenced by a number of factors, including the manager's perception of what motivates others (e.g. the stick/ carrot approach, consultation and participation, freedom, power) and the manager's own personality.

Both Kotter and Pugh highlight participative methods of management. These are Kotter's 'guiding coalition' and 'empowerment' step and Pugh's rules of informal discussion and the encouragement of objections. In Kotter's view, empowerment of employees should encourage risk-taking and non-traditional ideas. This is inappropriate for SMEs for two reasons. The first is that, although many small business owner/managers have taken risks (for example the initial risk to become self-employed), a smaller capital base leaves little room for business errors and will make managers of SMEs wary of taking risks for their own sake. In many cases, owner/managers will prefer to use tried and tested ideas unless the business is in severe trouble. The second problem with using Kotter's or Pugh's theory is that the dominant style of management within the pub sector is one of autocracy. Given that many of these businesses are run by owner/operators and are family businesses it is hardly surprising that an autocratic management style exists. Many owners of SMEs have put their personal savings into the business or used the family home as collateral to gain much-needed finance. Quite often the businesses are seen as an extension of the person him/herself and their control can be jealously guarded. In London's study of change agents he notes that '[some] successful entrepreneurs ... had trouble changing direction. Their view of corporate identity was entwined with their individual identity, and changing the corporation implied changing their self-concept' (1988, p. 52). Managers and owners who strongly identify themselves with the business may practise autocratic management styles because a perceived loss of control over the business implies loss of control in their life.

Speed of change

The speed of change in hospitality SMEs needs to be quick. This is particularly true of businesses operating on a seasonal basis or in a 'saturated' market. For example, if a competitor moves into a firm's market segment a decision needs to be taken quickly on whether to diversify the business or change the marketing strategy. When taking over a business, any change needs to be implemented swiftly to ensure minimum customer disruption and to reduce the possibility of 'sabotage' by disgruntled employees. Quite often there is little time to discuss such issues with workers.

Speed of change may also be an issue with employees. Staff used to working in a 'reactive' environment with pressurized customer service may expect a new manager or owner to make changes quickly. If change is implemented slowly it may strengthen or prolong feelings of job uncertainty, and this in turn may lead to demotivation and a diminished customer service.

Nature of employment and career prospects

Many HRM change-management texts (see London, 1988; Wilkinson, 1989; Kramar, McGraw and Schuler, 1997) seem preoccupied with large firms (for example, General Motors, Ford, Vauxhall Motors, AT&T, TSB Group, R&I Bank of Western Australia and the Woolwich Equitable Building Society). This is also the case with hospitality HRM texts (for example, Roberts, 1995). However, the nature of employment within the hospitality sector is markedly different from that of many of the companies mentioned above. Hospitality jobs tend to be part time and temporary rather than full time and year round. Seasonality plays a large part in this, with demand for labour increasing significantly during peak seasons. These labour demand patterns do little to build tangible career structures within individual SMEs. Instead, staff wishing for a career will need to move frequently amongst employers. Faced with this transient nature of employment, many experienced staff members are used to dealing with change in their working environment. In other words, if individuals are used to working part time, and/or on a temporary basis, the transition experienced when new managers or owners take over a team, or make significant organizational changes, is unlikely to be novel. Employees used to these types of working conditions are likely to accept change more readily and do not expect to be consulted, instead viewing change as an inevitable part of their working lives. While this type of working environment (autocratic management style, lack of career progression, flexible employment patterns) can be seen as being exploitative, it may not always be resented by employees.

Society is becoming less deferential, younger and better educated. Staff are therefore likely to demand that their voice is heard when managers make choices and decisions. However, it is also the case that for many workers, temporary, seasonal and part-time employment is a positive choice. Their leisure time or family may be important and work is just a means to an end – providing money to buy what they want. As Handy states:

The flexible labour force, in its turn, needs a different type of management. Without permanent constraints, with no possibility of promotion and no security, they cannot be expected to give the organization the kind of commitment and loyalty which one would hope to find in the core ... They are, after all, only there for the beer. (1992, p. 208)

It is important to remember that motivation is a personal construct. In other words, what motivates and is unacceptable to you (as an employee, manager or owner) may not necessarily affect others in the same way. As a thirty-something, middle-class, female, career-oriented, full-time manager, my views on employment and career progression will be somewhat different from those of a 25-year-old, mother of two, part-time bar person, or an 18-year-old, full-time student who works part time in a bar during term-time and full time during the summer vacation. Managers should, therefore, be aware of what motivates their staff and which management style is appropriate, and implement change management accordingly.

Major change-management theories fail to acknowledge the above diversity and assume that all staff, wherever they work, will respond positively to participative management and negatively to change. Differences in response to change could be a result of perceiving the change (or transition) as a 'normal' and therefore less stressful part of life. A knowledge of transition theory may help managers when managing change.

Transition theory

People experience many transitions during their lifetime – for example, from being at home to going to school; from going to school to starting work; from being single to being married (and back again); and many more besides. Some of these transitions are planned, expected and positive; others happen unexpectedly and cause pain and unhappiness. These experiences, to varying degrees, are likely to cause stress of some kind. Hopson defines a transition as 'a discontinuity in a person's life space' (1981, p. 225). This can be caused by a number of things (e.g. the death of a spouse; changing jobs), and can take place in one's personal or work life. Sometimes the discontinuity is defined by social consensus and thereby becomes recognized as a discontinuity within the culture. For example, the death of a spouse or the loss of one's job would generally be considered to be an important transition in our culture. Holmes and Rahe's social readjustment rating scale (1967) listed 43 life events in weighted order, the two most important being the death of a spouse and divorce. Work-related events were also rated highly: being fired was eighth; retiring was tenth; major business reorganization was fifteenth; and changing jobs was eighteenth.

However, Hopson also notes that another way to define a discontinuity in someone's life is by the person's perception of it. In other words, a person could perceive a transition differently from how another would perceive it. Hopson gives the following example:

> adolescence is considered to be an important time of transition in most western cultures, whereas in other cultures like Samoa it was not considered to be a time of stressful identity crisis. Also, in a common culture some children experience adolescence as a transition while others do not. (1981, p. 226)

As a consequence, he argues that we should not assume everyone experiences a transitional event in the same way. For an event to be classed as a transitional experience, there needs to be both a personal awareness of the discontinuity, and a new behavioural response because the situation is new, or the required behaviours are novel, or both (Hopson, 1981). A transition will result in people being affected to some degree by stress, but this will depend on the novelty of the situation they find themselves in. For example, a person choosing to work on a seasonal basis will find the transition to being unemployed in the off-season less problematic than a person who undertakes seasonal employment because it was the only job available. Being unemployed for long periods, the routine of 'signing-on', boredom, etc. will not be novel experiences, and the behaviour required to deal with them will not be new. Hopson points out that transitions are most stressful when they are unpredictable, involuntary, unfamiliar and have a high degree and rate of change. Hopson's model of transitions consists of a cycle of reactions and feelings that are predictable. The cycle has seven phases: immobilization, minimization, depression, letting go, testing, searching for meaning, and internalization. (See Table 8.2, p.146, for an explanation of the phases.) In short, individuals experience disruption; acknowledge its reality; test themselves and understand what it means; and incorporate the changes into their behaviour. Hopson argues that an individual will experience, to a lesser or greater degree, all of these phases of the transition. At the same time, a person's morale will change depending on where they are in the cycle; in addition, as each of us is unique, a person could become stuck in one phase or slip back to a previous phase, in some cases never moving on to the next phase of the cycle.

The importance of transition theory in managing change is to be aware of the cycle of reaction that change can cause. The notion that transitions cause differing reactions in individuals, depending on the novelty of the

Table 8.2 Hopson's model of transitions

Phase	Characteristics
Immobilization	Sense of being overwhelmed and unable to make plans.
	If the transition is not novel (for example, have experienced being fired before) or if the person has a positive expectation of the transition (for example, being promoted to manager), this is felt less intensely or not at all.
Minimization	The individual tries to minimize, disrupt, trivialize or deny the change exists. Sometimes the individual can project a feeling of euphoria.
	Denial can play an important part in the process, giving the individual time to retreat from reality and gain strength to deal with the new reality.
Depression	This may set in as people become aware of the new situation and the resultant changes they must make (for example, having to change one's lifestyle upon being made redundant).
	This phase can occur even when the transition has been voluntarily made. For example, an employee may decide to take early retirement but then become depressed as the reality that he or she has little to do all day sets in.
	Occasional high energy periods, characterized by anger, before returning to a feeling of hopelessness.
Letting go	Process of 'unhooking' from the past. The individual accepts the new reality for what it is.
	Optimism becomes possible. Acceptance that the change could be a 'blessing in disguise'.
Testing	The individual becomes more active and tries out new behaviours, lifestyles and ways of coping with the transition.
	Much personal energy available during this phase, which can result in anger and irritability.
Search for meaning	This is a cognitive process where the individual seeks to understand what the change has meant to his or her life.
Internalization	The meanings conceptualized in the phase above are internalized and incorporated into the individual's behaviour.

Adapted from: Hopson (1981)

transition, may give an insight into the reactions of staff within hospitality SMEs to the change procedure. In a highly flexible labour force that is used to changing work patterns and autocratic management styles, it is quite likely that any change effected by managers, and the resultant change in behaviour required, is not new. This may, therefore, make change less problematic and less stressful (for both staff and manager), and allow it to be effected speedily.

Team-building

Organizations are made up of people who have been formed into groups to carry out particular tasks. Within organizations there are both formal and informal groups. Formal groups are those constituted by management (and management selects the members, picks the leaders and chooses the method of work). They can be organized as a hierarchy, a network or a team (Bennett, 1989). Informal groups usually develop without the assistance or support of management and come about as members develop an affinity with each other, possess common interests and have a common cause. This section of the chapter focuses on a critique of team theories in relation to SMEs.

Bennett (1989, p. 110) defines a team as 'a special sort of group ... [whose] members cooperate and *voluntarily* coordinate their work in order to achieve group objectives'. He argues, therefore, that while a team is always a group, a group will not necessarily act as a team. One of the most influential writers on teams is Meredith Belbin (1992) who devised a list of eight roles essential for a good team. In brief they are as follows:

1. *Chairman*   calm self-confident and balanced. The chair's job is to pick the people, listen to and encourage them, and focus and co-ordinate the team's effort;

2. *Shaper*   highly motivated, extroverted and dynamic. The shaper's role is to lead the task, set priorities and deal with 'red tape'. He/she does not mind taking unpopular decisions;

3. *Plant*   creative, serious-minded, innovative. The plant is an 'ideas' person whose role is to generate new pro posals to solve complex problems. Plants tend to be introverted and inclined to disregard practical details;

4. *Resource investigator*   enthusiastic, extrovert, curious, good at communicating and negotiating. The resource investigator's
role is to liaise within the team and between the
team and the outside world;

5. *Monitor evaluator*   serious-minded, unemotional, prudent; likes to think
things over. His/her role is to weigh up the pros
and cons of any option;

6. *Company worker*   practical common sense, reliable, self-controlled,
predictable. Company workers are good organizers
and administrators who turn ideas into actions;

7. *Team worker*   sociable, popular, caring. The team worker's role is
to prevent interpersonal problems arising within the
team, thereby allowing all team members to contribute effectively;

8. *Completer finisher*   conscientious, accurate, orderly. His/her role is to
get the task done, usually within the deadlines set.
The completer finisher can be intolerant of those
with a more casual approach to life.

These eight roles do not need to be performed by eight different people. In general, people tend to have a secondary team role or characteristic. For example, using Belbin's 'self-perception inventory' (1992), I have a primary team role of a company worker, with a secondary role as a completer finisher. Therefore, with the 'right' people, the roles can be doubled up. In this way a team of four could cover all eight roles. However, Belbin suggests that six is a more appropriate size since this number allows for the chairman or the plant to focus solely on that role.

When teams are created they go through a period of development. The process has four stages: *forming, storming, norming* and *performing*. *Forming* is the initial process whereby the team creates its own identity and individuals find out the part they will play. *Storming* is when individuals begin to assert themselves and challenge the initial purpose or shape of the team. At the *norming* stage, the team settles down to the new way of working. Finally, upon maturity, the team begins to *perform*. It is argued (for example, see Handy, 1992) that teams cannot be expected to perform immediately when created. They need to undergo this process in order to build trust, and trust is needed in order for a team to work efficiently.

While Belbin and Handy look at the formation of teams, Bennett (1989) provides more practical advice on how to manage and build teams. He advises managers to:

- keep the teams small (no more than 12 people). This is because with a large team communication becomes difficult and the team requires more supervision;
- foster team spirit by implementing a participative management style. Participation improves morale and stimulates co-operation. Encourage joint decision-taking; praise and encourage members' suggestions for altering working methods, and never be sarcastic about suggestions;
- ensure someone is trained to take on the leadership role should you be promoted, leave the firm or be absent for long periods. If a group depends on a single person, there is a tendency for the team to collapse when its leader resigns;
- represent and defend the team in the outside world, and never criticize members in front of outsiders. The term 'outside world' includes other parts of the organization and the outside world itself;
- examine teams' status within the hierarchy of the organization and fight for resources for staff development;
- look at teams' physical work conditions (e.g. wage levels and terms and conditions of employment). Do the staff feel secure in their jobs?

Like change-management theories, Belbin's and Handy's team-building theories are problematic for managers of hospitality SMEs because they tend to focus on management teams rather than worker teams. In public house SMEs, the small number of employees will tend to discount the need for an organization to be formally departmentalized. It is less likely for there to be a management team at all. For instance, the manager or owner of a public house will usually undertake the management roles of marketing, sales, personnel, accounts, and purchasing. It is possible that there may be a bar manager or a catering manager, but the management team will most certainly be small. The type of team prevalent in hospitality SMEs, therefore, is an operational one, i.e. made up of operational staff (the 'workers').

In a highly pressurized customer service environment, the skills most required from staff are practical personal skills, speed and dexterity. Operational teams would therefore be better peopled by one or two company and team workers, and several completer finishers. While there is no doubt that the other team roles could play a valuable part in such a team, the work environment (pace, seasonality, flexible labour patterns and management style) would make it difficult for operational staff to be able to expand their roles to encompass, for example, monitor evaluator or plant tasks.[3] When a pub is open, the staff are busy serving customers; when a pub is shut or not busy the staff are put to work in preparation for serving customers, for example by 'bottling-up', preparing food, cleaning and checking the spirit dispensers. These are operational tasks that require completing in a timely fashion. Rarely will a manager during quiet times or before opening hours ask a member of staff to stop performing operational tasks and instead, in a monitor evaluator role, sit and think about how he or she could serve customers better. Operational teams do not have the time to form, storm, norm and then perform. Managers of hospitality SMEs, particularly pubs and hotels in seasonal resorts, need operational teams to perform from the moment the staff are hired. These SMEs, with a limited time to make money, literally cannot afford to have a period of under-performance.

Bennett's more practical suggestions regarding team-building cause problems for managers of SMEs because of the underlying need for participative management styles within teams to make them work. It has already been pointed out above that a participative management style is unusual within the hospitality SME sector. Bennett too bases his theory around larger organizations.

CONCLUSION AND RECOMMENDATIONS FOR MANAGING CHANGE AND TEAM-BUILDING

Managers inheriting staff need to manage the change process and build a team. Often when taking over a business this can mean structural reorganization and the sacking of staff (particularly if staff are deemed to be 'badly' trained). However, the sacking of inadequately trained staff need not occur if the new manager is prepared to retrain them to his or her standards. The owner/manager will also need to implement team-building to mould the group to the new standards, values and goals. This is especially the case for managers who take over a team rather than the business as a whole, since full scale reorganization is unlikely in these cases.

Several change-management and team-building theories have been advanced to help with the above processes. However, they are aimed specifically at large organizations and in the area of team roles, and apply to managers rather than workers. Nevertheless, some aspects of the theories, adjusted to meet SMEs' requirements, could provide a useful framework for managers to work within.

Recommendations

In the area of change management, Pugh's (1986) six point plan makes practical suggestions on how to implement change. As with other change-management theories, participative management is seen as the key to instigating change. Those involved in the change should be encouraged to give their views in order to make them feel part of the process and less likely to resist the change. However, participative management styles may not work in an environment unused to such a way of working. Staff used to a more autocratic style of management may react suspiciously to a new management technique. Managers should also be aware that some workers, perhaps those on seasonal contracts or those working part time with no long-term career prospects, may not care to be involved in decision-making or giving their views.

Some practical advice for managing the change process includes:

- think through the change, taking into account what it will mean to others. This will help you identify any points of resistance. However, recognize that those involved in the change may have differing expectations from you, and for some, the transition may not be novel. Think about how this may affect the speed of change and the staff's reaction to it;
- where possible practise participative management by encouraging feedback and informal discussions. However, be aware that for some staff, participative management techniques will have little effect. You may, therefore, need to use more than one management style;
- implement the change quickly, i.e. have a reasonably short timescale for the change process from start to finish. Small businesses generally need to react quickly to the stimulus for change, so the change process itself should reflect this. In this way the period of uncertainty felt by staff during the change process should be lessened, and with it, the potential for poor customer service caused by absenteeism, bad time-keeping, 'sabotage' etc.;
- be prepared to change yourself. This includes both your views (if an employee comes up with a better idea than yours) and your personal convictions (management style, goals and values);
- be aware of the effect changes have on people (transition theory) and the stage of the process your staff (and you) may be at. Think about the different motivational techniques that may be needed during each part of the transition process;
- finally, be prepared to have negative feelings as well as positive ones

during the change process. Even though you may be doing what is right for the business, you may have acted 'badly' in the staff's interests, for example, having to sack staff. This may be more keenly felt in hospitality SMEs where staffing levels are low and managers tend to work alongside staff in an operational role.

Team-building theories tend to be based on large organizations; concentrate on management teams (Belbin (1992) in particular); and focus on building new teams rather than taking over the leadership of an existing team. Although Bennett (1989) appears to have based his ideas around large organizations, he does provide some practical advice on team-building that could be applied in SMEs, and I would recommend that you read his chapter entitled 'Managing a team'. Further recommendations are:

- when deciding on a deputy to carry out your team leader role, be aware that this can cause problems within the team. You may have decided to pick a particular person because of the skills and attributes you perceive that person to have. However, other team members may feel the decision has arisen out of paternalism or favouritism. Communicate your reason for the decision, perhaps by making a formal announcement at the beginning of a shift or by putting a note up on the staff notice board (if you have one);
- if the staff are new to you, carry out an informal appraisal with each member of staff. This can take the form of a brief chat, preferably somewhere quiet and private. Although this may be time consuming, and will require planning for the disruption in staffing levels, it can be a valuable way of finding out about your new staff (their skills, abilities, hopes and fears), and a good source of new ideas and work-related gossip;
- be prepared during this conversation to tell the staff something about yourself. Do not give them your life story – it is important to keep things on a professional level – but do give them a brief history of your work experience, and explain any new ideas you may have. This may help you to 'win the team over'. Remember, they have been used to working for another manager, one who may have had quite a different style from you or quite different ideas. One way of pushing a team towards taking on new values and norms is if the person leading the team is seen to have 'expert' knowledge or personal charisma.

Notes

1 These figures therefore discount the large chain operations such as Harvester Restaurants or Beefeater, because their predominant business is not selling beer.
2 This is where the owner/managers (publicans) have bought the 'in-goings' (fixtures and fittings, stock, equipment etc.) from the previous publican and pay the brewery a rent for the premises.
3 It would be hoped that the manager could provide the roles of chairman, plant, shaper, resource investigator and monitor evaluator. However, most of us have a propensity towards one or two roles at most. From this it can be seen that it is unlikely that one manager could carry out all these roles. This could have a significant impact on SMEs with very small management teams.

REFERENCES

Belbin, R. M. (1992), *Management Teams: Why They Succeed or Fail*. Oxford: Butterworth-Heinemann.

Bennett, R. (1989), *Managing People*. London: Kogan Page.

Blunt, S. (1995), All change for the new century! *Innkeeper Year Book 1995*. British Institute of Innkeeping, p. 89.

Hampson, T. (1998), Brewers, Licensee and Retailers Association, personal communication 26 August.

Handy, C. (1992), *Inside Organizations: 21 Ideas for Managers*. London: BBC Books.

Holmes, T. H. and Rahe, R. H. (1967), The social readjustment rating scale. *Journal of Psychosomatic Research*, **11**, 213–18.

Hopson, B. (1981), Transition: understanding and managing personal change. In L. C. Cooper (ed.), *Psychology and Management: A Text for Managers and Trade Unionists*. London and Basingstoke: The British Psychological Society and Macmillan Press, pp. 225–49.

Kotter, J. P. (1995), *Leading Change*. Cambridge, MA: Harvard Business School Press.

Kotter, J. P. and Schlesinger, L. A. (1986), Choosing strategies for change. In

B. Mayon-White (ed.), *Planning and Managing Change*. London: Harper & Row, pp. 160–72.

Kramar, R., McGraw, P. and Schuler, R. S. (1997), *Human Resource Management in Australia*, 3rd edn. Australia: Longman.

Labour Market Data (1988), *Employment Gazette*, November, p. S12.

Labour Market Data (1998), *Labour Market Trends*, January, p. S13.

Lee-Ross, D. (1996), A study of attitudes and work motivation among seasonal hotel workers. PhD thesis, Cambridge, Anglia Polytechnic University.

London, M. (1988), *Change Agents: New Roles and Innovation Strategies for Human Resource Professionals*. San Francisco: Jossey-Bass Publishers.

Lupton, T. (1986), Organizational change: 'Top-down' or 'bottom-up' management? In B. Mayon-White (ed.), *Planning and Managing Change*, London: Harper & Row, pp. 55–66.

Mars, G. and Nicod, M. (1984), *The World of Waiters*. London: Allen and Unwin.

Pugh, D. (1986), Understanding and managing organizational change. In B. Mayon-White (ed.), *Planning and Managing Change*. London: Harper & Row, pp. 141–5.

Purcell, K. and Quinn, J. (1995), *Hospitality Management Education and Employment Trajectories*. Oxford: Oxford Brookes University.

Radiven, N. and Lucas, R. (1996), The abolition of wages councils and its impact on the pay policy of small businesses in the hotel industry. *Conference Proceedings*, IAHMS Spring Symposium, Leeds Metropolitan University, UK, pp. 143–51.

Roberts, J. (1995), *Human Resource Practice in the Hospitality Industry*. London: Hodder & Stoughton.

Stevenson, W. C. (1986), *Making and Managing a Pub*. London: David & Charles.

Wilkinson, T. (1989), *All Change at Work: The Human Dimension*. London: Institute of Personnel Management.

Wright, S. (1984), *Running Your Own Pub*. London: Hutchinson & Co.

CHAPTER NINE

HRM Case Studies in Tourism SMEs

Nick Johns and Szilvia Gyimóthy

INTRODUCTION

The task of selecting representative case studies of small to medium-sized tourism enterprises (SMEs) is fraught with difficulties. In the first place 'tourism' potentially includes shopping and business trips as well as 'touristic' visits, all of which rely upon different types of service provision. Services intended for tourists also conspicuously include lodging and refreshments, yet in many ways it is convenient to separate the two. In this chapter, businesses oriented towards tourism are considered to be those which contribute directly to holidays; represent a local speciality of some sort; or provide some kind of amenity for 'tourists' (tentatively defined as outsiders to the region in question). Among these, three specific areas can be identified: catering, transport and attractions. The cases presented here are drawn from these three types.

Even more daunting is the challenge of selecting representative business types and employment structures. Tourism SMEs are often identified as traditional, family-owned operations, originally frequently reliant upon extended family structures. As families have shrunk and scattered, the businesses have had to devise ways of bringing in staff to fulfil many of the day-to-day tasks, but have retained as much control in the core family as possible. However, many small tourism businesses are of mixed ownership, or operate as more or less independent, wholly-owned subsidiaries of public sector organizations. Such businesses are 'small' in relation to the size of their workforce, and often highly market-oriented and professionally designed. This diversity thus raises the question of whether small in terms of numbers is an appropriate catch-all term for such different organizational types. The tourism small business sector has its full share of the full-time, part-time, permanent and casual work patterns mentioned earlier in this book. Besides this, volunteers may be involved in delivering the sector's core product, particularly if this includes heritage re-enactment.

This chapter presents three cases, which aim to provide a broad overview of employment in small to medium-sized tourism businesses. These are as follows:

1. a traditional family-owned fish smoke house on the Danish resort island of Bornholm, run as a family business with labour supplements from the island itself and further afield. This business is strictly seasonal and the family is not closely involved with visitors;
2. a family-owned boatyard catering to holidaymakers on the Norfolk Broads (UK). This business is broadly seasonal, with a 'shoulder' period and some winter hiring. Local labour is used on a casual basis only, and the family is closely involved in all aspects of the business;
3. a heritage attraction in Wales (UK) run as an independent subsidiary of a county council. This business runs on a year-round basis with about 30 locally recruited employees, and a supplement of casual staff and volunteers.

Permission was obtained to give two of these cases, Gudhjem Smokery and Llancaiach Fawr, their real names. 'Black's Boatyard' does not in fact exist, although its features can be found at two different yards, much as they are described here. This amalgamation has made it possible to provide anonymity as requested and also to make the case somewhat richer than it otherwise would have been. The three cases are presented separately and discussed at the end of the chapter in terms of issues arising in several other chapters of this book, including:

- the employment environment;
- organizational issues;
- administration;
- nature of work;
- motivation;
- team-working.

The objective is to demonstrate the universality of many of these issues in the small to medium-sized business sector, but also to allow the reader to appreciate both the diversity of the area and those aspects that are distinctive to the 'tourism' area.

CASES

Gudhjem Fish Smokery, Bornholm, Denmark

The enterprise

The Island of Bornholm is a Danish resort situated in the Baltic, about 100 miles east of Copenhagen. It has a resident population of about 45,000, traditionally engaged in agriculture and fishing, together with the service infrastructure needed to support a relatively isolated community. However, during the summer months, some 600,000 holiday visitors come to the island. Attractions available to them include heritage sites such as the famous round churches, built by the Baltic Crusaders, the sixteenth century Hammershus castle, museums and galleries, beaches, nature reserves, and shops selling arts and crafts.

Fish smokeries were introduced to Bornholm by Scottish fishermen in the seventeenth century. They proved a popular way to preserve herrings, one of the Danish staple foods. During the past two hundred years, Bornholm smoked herrings have become a regional delicacy of Danish cuisine, and the smoke houses (with their distinctive, pyramidal chimneys) are now one of the island's traditional industries. Like most such operations (and like many small tourism-related businesses elsewhere) Gudhjem Fish Smokery is a family-owned business. Its activities include fish and seafood processing, smoking and direct sales. The owner (third generation in the smoke house business) deals with various managerial tasks, such as organizing raw material purchase, human resource recruitment, accounting, promotion, etc. Like other Bornholm smokeries, Gudhjem Fish Smokery represents local fast-food restaurant provision, providing inexpensive food in a rustic environment (wooden benches, no table-cloths, paper plates and plastic forks). With its typical smoke house chimneys, woodpile and simple aspect it blends well with its surroundings. The food itself is simple, but is of good quality, healthy, tasty and carries the added attraction of being a local speciality.

Employment structure

There are two main job areas: fish-smoking and sales. Four of the fish smokers are local, middle-aged males, who previously worked in the fishing industry, but some members of the family also do this work. The job includes cleaning and preparing the fish, smoking them, and bringing the finished product to the cold store. Smoking is kept separate from sales operations, both physically and temporally (i.e. in a building next door to the restaurant and early in the morning, before customers begin to arrive). The number of sales employees varies slightly with the time of year and with the availability of personnel. There are generally five or six, mostly female, aged 18–26 years. Although they tend to come from other parts of Denmark, they nearly always have some sort of ties (family or friends) with Bornholm. Their job includes preparing smoked fish and seafood for sale, serving portions for groups, selling food and drinks and cleaning up. Sales employees normally work ten to twelve hours a day during the season (May to October) without a weekly day off. For some this stretches for the whole of the season, but more usually it is from late-June to mid-August, when the largest number of employees is needed.

There is no real hierarchy in either job area. Experienced sales employees tend to act as supervisors or mentors, guiding new members of staff and helping them to learn the daily routine. New staff are generally entrusted with the less exciting tasks, such as cleaning tables, or bringing out fresh food from the store-room. The time it takes individuals to become experienced or rise in the pecking order depends upon their diligence and aptitude. The atmosphere is very stressful during main meal times, but also has its lighter side in the form of running repartee between the bar and the fish counter. Membership of the experienced staff sector allows one to participate in these small jokes and remarks. The owner/manager does not take part in the daily operation of the restaurant, and does not attempt to control it. Monitoring of the sales people is the responsibility of the most experienced employee, who prepares the daily work-plan, looks after the book-keeping and assumes general control. She also works full time as an ordinary sales employee, and this tends to produce considerable role stress. Because of the fatigue this position brings, it is usually undertaken by the same individual for a maximum of only two consecutive seasons.

The daily routine at Gudhjem Fish Smokery is defined by a work-plan, usually drawn up each previous evening. The plan includes the allocation of work (sales at the counter, preparation of portions and salads, cleaning up etc.), so that staff can rotate between different functions. If there is a larger group booked in for the next day, all staff must work hard in the morning to be ready with the portions required. Mealtime rush hours are 12.00–14.00 and from 17.00 onwards, and at these times there is increased pressure on sales employees. The main source of conflict originates from the speed of service, especially during rush hours. Holiday visitors tend to take their time over choosing what to eat. Menus are in Danish and sometimes a lack of translated information can also cause delays. As a result, long queues build up in front of the counter. This irritates sales employees, who perceive their job as serving people quickly, smoothly and effectively. When customers have ordered their food, they have to queue again to order drinks, bringing another source of irritation.

Employee recruitment

Gudhjem Fish Smokery has a core list of fish-smoking employees who tend to be to re-employed year after year. However, because of the high demand for personnel during the tourist season, engaging suitable sales employees presents a more acute problem. This is solved through three main routes:

- *word of mouth* through friends or relatives around the island. These frequently will know someone, who lives elsewhere in Denmark, but is willing to work on Bornholm (one of the most attractive resort islands) during the summer months;
- *formal recruitment channels* In Denmark this means calling the local job centre. However, it is a highly unionized country. There is also the possibility of contacting the restaurateurs' trade union;
- *advertising* is usually through the local newspaper, although community notice-boards may also be used. It is not generally thought necessary to advertise further afield, as the individuals most likely to come are those who already have close connections with the island.

The transient employees recruited in this way are referred to locally as 'butterflies' and most of them are students working during the summer months. They usually return to the smokery two or three years in a row, motivated by ready cash and the young and dynamic environment. None of the staff is required to provide evidence of previous vocational training and when staff are recruited, assumptions about their personal hygiene, social and practical skills are mostly made on the basis of their appearance and first impression.

Training, promotion and salary

The smokery provides no training because it regards the tasks as very simple, and staff turnover is high. On the first day, beginners are given an apron and shown around the premises. They are instructed in basic operational routines, such as preparation of food and salads and use of the till, and told the prices of the fish. After this they begin work behind the fish counters. The beverage bar serves soft drinks and beer and is usually operated by an experienced employee.

There are no steady patterns of staff development or promotion. If staff seem motivated and suitable, they may be regarded as 'responsible' after just one season. Nor are there any pay differentials or monetary incentives. Sales employees are paid an hourly DKK100 (UK£9.06, US$14.84 at the time of writing). This is considered to be a relatively good wage for students, but is subject to a high rate of national income tax. Everyone, even the most senior of the 'experienced' sales employees, receives the same salary. Tipping is rare in Denmark, and there is no system or practice for pooling tips or sharing them between staff. Employees leave when they feel that the trade-off between the salary and the work-load is no longer worthwhile, or else they finish their studies and the summer job loses its attraction.

Black's Boatyard, Norfolk, UK

The enterprise

The Norfolk and Suffolk Broads are a system of largely man-made lakes, linked by fenland and rivers and located in the most easterly part of England, close to the North Sea coast. The area was opened up as a tourist destination during the late-nineteenth and early-twentieth century, and has since become a popular boating centre for domestic holiday-makers. The usual pattern for visitors from outside the region is to rent a boat for one or two weeks and to tour the Broads system, stopping at pubs, towns and attractions along the way. Locals and casual tourists may hire day boats for shorter, self-drive tours. Besides the joys of the boating life, there are numerous attractions to visit, including a bygone village, museums and heritage sites in Norwich, Caister and other towns. There are also visitor information centres and nature reserves.

Many of the existing Norfolk boat-yards were set up during the 1920s and 1930s, when motor boats dropped to affordable prices and holiday-makers found themselves able to rent them. Originally, boat-yard workers built and maintained their own craft. However, the years since 1945 have seen a steady growth in specialized boat-building, particularly for the holiday boating industry. Modern cruisers bear little resemblance to the rather Spartan hire craft of the mid-twentieth century. They are fibreglass in construction, and designed for maximum comfort and ease of cleaning and maintenance (so that, for example, hulls and interiors need little in the way of repainting or re-varnishing). The main operational demands are cleaning and mechanical maintenance. Broads' boat-yards traditionally hire from Saturday to Saturday, and this places a considerable burden on cleaning and running maintenance, which frequently has to be accomplished within a twelve hour weekly 'window'. The Broads season lasts from the UK late May Bank Holiday (usually the last week in May) until the end of August. However, there are important and growing 'shoulder seasons' from Easter onwards, and from September until late October. The boats are so comfortably appointed that it is even possible to hire them during the winter period, for example, over Christmas.

Black's Boatyard is a family-run business owned by two brothers (whose grandfather started building and hiring boats in the 1920s). They operate a fleet of thirty craft (now purchased from local specialist boat-builders) including both cabin cruisers and day boats. The operation entails booking customers and attending to their needs while they are on holiday, and cleaning and mechanically maintaining the boats. Black's Boatyard issues information packs assembled and distributed by Norfolk Attractions Association, of which the yard is a member. These include maps of the Broads and details of local attractions. In addition holiday-makers can buy various novelty goods and souvenirs in the small boat-yard shop.

Employment structure

The two brothers and the wife of one of them (the other brother is unmarried) run the boat-yard on a day-to-day basis. The wife undertakes administrative tasks such as customer and financial records, purchasing, staffing and a limited amount of marketing. The brothers look after the boats (in terms of maintenance, repair, emergencies, registration etc.). All three family members take turns to staff the office and greet customers, and the brothers take new customers out for a 'driving lesson' to familiarize them with boat handling and safety.

Employment centres around cleaning the boats, and tends to be concentrated into the weekends, mostly between Friday evening and Saturday afternoon. At this time a variable number of casual workers come in (usually about eight, but this depends upon work-load and availability). If enough casuals cannot be found, family members take a hand in this work. The boating holiday season coincides both with a peak demand for casual staff and with school holiday times. For this reason few individuals work for a complete season, and it is necessary to have a large 'book' of potential applicants, from which to call in emergencies. Casual workers used in this way are of two main types. About half are young, are still at school or college, or have just left school and not yet found employment. They may be of either sex, but females are preferred, because they are considered to have a greater knowledge of, and aptitude for, cleaning. The other half are middle-aged, married women – preferred by the boat-yard because they are more stable and permanent, generally understand the job well, and often can be called upon for several consecutive years. Cleaning work is assigned to individuals in terms of a number of boats that need to be serviced. The job includes mopping, vacuum-cleaning, and checking and correcting the cleanliness of crockery, cutlery, cookware, bed-linen and so on. In addition certain basic supplies are replenished and a few complimentary items are provided for the boat customers. Work has to be completed with great speed and efficiency, otherwise customers may complain about waiting for boats or about their condition. Allocation schedules are rudimentary, drawn up by the wife (who also directs the cleaning operation) according to the number of boats scheduled for hire. More experienced cleaners act to some extent as mentors for inexperienced (and particularly for young) ones.

Employee recruitment

Black's Boatyard already has a large list of casual staff, built up over several years' operation. These are predominantly recruited by word of mouth. Local people hear about the opportunity, apply to the yard for jobs and are added to the list. Also parents may apply on behalf of their student offspring who wish to earn holiday money. Sometimes the yard also advertises through the *Norfolk Daily Press* or through cards pinned to notice-boards in local shops.

On the whole recruitment is less of a problem than actually managing employee availability on a daily or weekly basis. At weekends there is frequently a 'panic stations' situation as increasingly frantic telephone calls are made to increasingly unlikely prospects.

Training, promotion and salary

Black's Boatyard does not regard training as part of its staffing policy. Its employees work on a casual basis and there is high turnover, at least in formal terms (in practice, individuals tend to leave and return erratically). In any case, the work is not regarded as complicated or skilled. When new casuals come they accompany a more experienced worker, on a 'sitting by Nellie' basis, until they are judged to have grasped the essentials. After this they are allocated boats of their own to clean. As with most casual work, opportunities for promotion or self-development are neither provided nor expected. The rate of pay is £3.80 (US$ 6.22) per hour for a school-leaver at the time of writing, but older workers receive up to £4.50 (US$ 7.37) per hour. This is regarded as reasonable, and even good, in an area known for depressed wages and high seasonal unemployment.

Llancaiach Fawr Living History Museum, Wales, UK

Llancaiach Fawr Living History Museum, located in unspoiled farmland in the heart of the South Wales valleys, operates as a wholly-owned independent subsidiary of Caerphilly County Borough Council. Its centrepiece is a semi-fortified manor house, built in 1530, which has been restored to the style of its heyday and is used to celebrate the life and times of Colonel Edward Prichard, a local hero of the English Civil War. Llancaiach Fawr's mission is to enable visitors to understand the life ordinary people lived during 1645, an arbitrarily chosen date from that period. In order to do this, both traditional and live interpretative techniques are used. For example, actors in period costume re-enact life at the manor house, taking on the roles of historical persons. They represent a typical gentleman's household (both family and servants) of the time and act, speak, and are dressed in seventeenth-century style. Characters portrayed include Captain Bolitto (a rascally knave) and Ann Thomas, the gossiping housekeeper. In order to make the visitor's time journey still more realistic, all interfaces with the modern world are located at a distance from the manor house. These include both the visitor facilities and visitor information (about the house and the historical background of the exhibits) which is provided before guests enter the main part of the attraction.

The furniture and furnishings in the manor house are reproduction, and so visitors can be invited to try them out and the only operational cost is normal wear and tear. In effect, the site offers a 'hands-on museum', in which visitors (especially children) can explore different activities. These include pomander- and candle-making, cheese tasting, and seventeenth-century games and dances. The dramatization of documented history in such a relaxed, entertaining environment provides good value for money because visitors can experience first hand the tastes, smells, sounds and speech patterns of Stuart times. In addition to the manor house there is a shop selling novelty items and artefacts, and a small museum, which aims to prepare visitors for the 'time-warp' experience in the main part of the exhibit. There are teaching rooms and equipment, which are used by visiting school parties, and also for staff training. Over the years Llancaiach

Fawr has built up impressive catering facilities. A conservatory dining area and space for banqueting and functions have been added to the original small, informal café-restaurant.

The manor house has operated on a year-round basis since it opened in the early 1990s, and has received over 150,000 visitors within its first three years of operation (Waycott, 1995). It has gained a number of prestigious tourist board awards, including best new attraction and best family attraction, as well as education awards. Tudor and Stuart history is a compulsory part of the UK national curriculum in schools, and the Living History Museum is in constant demand for school visits. The Llancaiach Fawr manor house has become a fountainhead of regional rejuvenation, since it effectively acts as a flagship attraction. After almost a decade of operation, it has managed to change people's perceptions of the Welsh valleys, attracting visitors from all over the UK. These, in turn, have discovered the beauty of the countryside, and benefit the local tourism industry in increasing numbers (Waycott, 1995). The essence of Llancaiach Fawr is its atmosphere. Maintaining the impression of a seventeenth-century time-warp is hard work, and actor–interpreters must concentrate upon staying in character. They are trained to 'forget' all that has happened since 1645, and all of the emphasis is on a light-hearted, but essentially accurate, immersion in the period. The museum's informal mission statement could be 'from hard work to magic'.

Employment structure

At the time of writing, Llancaiach Fawr has 32 employees, divided between three notional 'departments': interpretation (12 staff), catering (8 staff) and administration–reception (10 staff). The third department includes staff engaged in the shop and in general maintenance of the site. These numbers do not include extra unemployed persons attached to the operation under the national (UK) 'New Deal Initiative'. In addition to these permanent employees, Llancaiach Fawr employs a number of casual service staff to meet the extra demands of banquets and functions. As elsewhere, this involves keeping a list of likely individuals and making a large number of phone calls as the need arises. There is a retail outlet on site run by a local handcraft business that also sells Stewart Crystal on a concessionary basis.

Volunteers

Volunteers are recruited for the summer months (and for special events) via contacts or newspaper advertisements asking whether readers would like to 'live as a Tudor'. They have to undergo interviews and training as employees do. Volunteers are given extensive notes on the costume and shoes of the period, from which they must make their own costumes. No subsidies are provided for the cost of the costumes. Over the years since it opened, the museum has built up a core of expertise among its volunteers and it can now call on teams of specialists. For example, a team of musketeers regularly provides weaponry demonstrations.

Recruitment

All employees and volunteers are recruited from the local catchment area. In principle divisions exist between categories of staff and between the type of work staff are expected to do. However, in practice a system of job rotation and an ethos of 'mucking in together' tend to iron out such distinctions. Most applicants are drawn to the museum by an interest in history or theatre. For the first two years of operation, Llancaiach Fawr relied upon the specialist firm Past Pleasures (a leading company in the interpretation field) for assistance with the recruitment of live interpreters. The company acted as a consultant, weeding out unsuitable applicants, sitting in on interviews and participating in the subsequent selection process. However, the museum soon decided to break down all distinctions between the different categories of staff and instituted its own recruitment procedures for all applicants.

Training of interpretation staff

Llancaiach Fawr's success depends upon the uniqueness of the product, upon its innovative and positive approach, and also upon the effectiveness of the actor–interpreters. Interpretation staff play a key role in the impact of the site, and therefore have to be highly skilled and knowledgeable. Each new recruit receives a two-week programme of intensive training which provides him or her with the necessary historical background and also the skills for the job. In order to carry out historical interpretation effectively, it is important to enable visitors temporarily to suspend their disbelief and enter a time-warp in which they achieve a sense of actually being in another time. The goal of training is to make employees confidently convincing in their role, so that the public believes what they say. They must also be able to acquire the skill of deflecting questions to which they do not know the answer or which are intended to challenge authenticity (for example, 'Isn't that an aeroplane up there?'), and to avoid stepping out of their allotted role, even for a moment.

Following the two-week intensive course, actor–interpreters receive additional ongoing training, which includes deportment, period knowledge (i.e. costume, speech, manners, social history) and the Welsh language. They are also allowed one day per month for personal research, during which they can develop their character roles and devise new story lines. Rotation between different character roles helps to protect staff from stress and to shield them from actor burn-out. In addition, it is Llancaiach Fawr's policy to rotate staff between departments, so that all staff, no matter what their job, spend time working in other areas to understand what the others are doing. Someone who is mainly located in the administrative 'department' for instance can expect to take an interpretive role for a day, or to act as a food-server or a cleaner, if the need arises. This helps to develop a strong cohesiveness and team spirit among all staff at the museum. It also helps develop an understanding of what is operationally practicable. For example, after spending some days in the manor house, a receptionist will not book a group of 50 visitors half an hour before closing on a Friday evening. All employees, including the actor–interpreters, receive wider training, which includes customer care. Like most Welsh tourism organizations, Llancaiach Fawr has adopted the Welcome Host Wales scheme, managed by the Welsh tourist board. This aims to provide consistent standards of customer service, care and hospitality throughout the region.

Initial training programmes were arranged and delivered by the specialist historical interpretation company Past Pleasures. However, the museum rapidly became aware of its own interpretational and training needs. After the second year of operation, Llancaiach Fawr set up its own training programmes and now acts as a regional consultant to other aspiring living history centres.

DISCUSSION

The employment environment

The three cases presented here cannot be considered entirely representative of the sector. Tourist services may be found in cities and urban areas, whereas these three cases are all rurally located. A substantial proportion of small tourism businesses are, however, based in the countryside, and to this extent these cases are typical. In such situations, there is often a seasonal cycle of labour availability, with competition between the declining, but still substantial, needs of agriculture (for example the harvesting of fruit or vegetables) and the growing industries based on tourism. Much of the British countryside still has a sufficient population to meet these needs. However, in less populous areas (Bornholm is typical of many islands of Europe and the UK in this respect), labour mobility and availability present a problem. This is exacerbated by a general and probably accurate perception within the industry that customers wish to be served by 'real locals' (Gyimothy, forthcoming). Local recruitment becomes much less of a problem when, like Llancaiach Fawr, attractions can operate all year round, spread the demand for personnel over all seasons, and at the same time offer their staff a level of job security.

The pattern portrayed in the three cases, of family-run traditional businesses versus newer concerns sponsored by local government, is a fairly general one, especially in rural areas of Europe. Many of the UK's independent museums and heritage attractions were set up in the 1980s with the help of Manpower Services Commission money, and deployed the young unemployed in the preservation of local heritage sites. Other areas of Europe have since seen parallel developments, and subsequent business trends towards organizational de-layering and de-structuring have left many of them in a similar position to Llancaiach Fawr. Middleton (1990) notes the intensifying competition that such attractions faced in the recession of the late-1980s and early-1990s, when an increasing number of sites found themselves competing for dwindling levels of visitor spending. It is interesting that Llancaiach Fawr is again supporting and training unemployed individuals under the British Government's 1997 New Deal scheme. Although such initiatives benefit individuals and communities in the short term, it seems that subsidization of labour and training in this way must inevitably accustom the tourist industry to cheaper labour, and ultimately to lower rates of pay.

More established tourist service operations are typically run by local families. In rural areas this often means those with a farming connection, since such families have traditionally owned surplus capital in the form of land and buildings, and possess the skills necessary for rural crafts. In the case of Black's Boatyard, the family also had the mechanical skills necessary for maintaining the boats. At the Gudhjem Smokery the family originally operated fishing boats. However, families may sometimes also buy small, low capital tourist operations of this kind from their own resources, and this tends to dilute the local influence.

Organizational and administrative issues

Family-run businesses are often motivated by very different considerations from the predominantly economic motives of larger organizations. These include the quality of life, as well as care and consideration for family members, and they tend to manifest themselves in idiosyncratic organizational structures and management styles (see for example, Kozak and Rimmington, 1998). This can be seen in the very different running of Black's Boatyard and the Gudhjem Smokery. In each case the family seems to have taken over areas in which they were personally interested, and then hired employees to fulfil the other tasks.

As with small businesses in most other sectors, management activities are often carried out in an intuitive or even *ad hoc* manner. For instance the authors were once shown a section of wall in the hallway of a business premises with the words ' . . . and this is my personnel department'. On this wall were posted a number of notes with names and telephone numbers: the casuals who were to be rung for cleaning duties the next day. To some extent this is dictated by the small scale of the enterprises, and by the loneliness of running a business in isolation from any perceivable mainstream of management practice. Nonetheless, these *ad hoc* initiatives tend to build up into unwieldy customs and practices, where 'fire fighting' is the norm. There is little room for reflection, or for the development of coherent policies, and the predominant organizational strategy is surviving to the next season. The apparent disorder in operational and strategic management does not necessarily imply that family-based small businesses lack managerial competencies. An alternative explanation for day-to-day operations could be that these enterprises take pride in being and staying small, and do not strive for expansion. A rural accommodation provider, for example, was well aware of the competitiveness and uniqueness of his offering:

> I think our guests mainly like being on a working farm, they like to see the hubbub and the activity of a farm going on around them; the animals, the smelling or making the noise, and most of all they like the informality of it. The rates which we charge are well below hotel rates, but we consider the service and the facilities which we provide are superior. The family gives them a cracking great big breakfast which they wouldn't get in a hotel. (Quoted in Waycott, 1995)

It might be argued then, that businesses staying small and successful on their own choice would not easily fit into the 'accepted' organizational life-cycle model.

This bleak picture of operational chaos, however, can be tempered with experience from Gudhjem Fish Smokery and from Llancaiach Fawr. The pressures described above undoubtedly exist in both of these sites, but at Gudhjem Smokery, the owner is able to distance himself to some extent from the day-to-day running of the operation. Thus there is potential for reflection and strategic development. The owner is currently investing in catering outlets around the island and striving to enlarge the family business. Llancaiach Fawr is in somewhat of a different position, since it is not a family-run enterprise. Managers are hired, and can be fired if they do not perform. They may also draw upon management experience from within local government circles. In any case heritage is a new, vibrant field with its own literature and a growing ethos of innovation, and this can constantly refresh management thinking.

Service quality

In late twentieth-century tourism, as in many other service industries, the customer's concept of quality is changing rapidly. Technological advances have brought the development of communication networks and, in the wake of the internet, an increasing desire for personal interaction rather than the mere witnessing of historical or other artefacts. The nineteenth-century awe of the artefact that can be viewed (museums), hired (boats), or consumed (smoked fish) has largely disappeared, and has been replaced by a desire for 'hands-on' interaction concepts. Thus quality has been displaced from the exhibit to the exhibitor, but this is not always recognized as such by traditional small tourism businesses. The lesson from these cases is the huge role that front-line personnel play in service quality, by 'generating' the visitor experience and filling a gap left by a paradigmatic shift in social perceptions of location and history.

According to current marketing theory (see, for example, Berry and Parasuraman, 1991) the quality of a service experience (such as that of a holiday visitor) determines both customer satisfaction/dissatisfaction and the likelihood of a return visit. In the twenty-first century perhaps the degree of interaction, and level of engrossment in a heritage presentation, will be a measure of its quality. The ability of tourist services to interrupt the continuity of customers' twentieth-century reality, and to illuminate a familiar yet new perspective of the past, will perhaps become the focus of quality concepts. Although this is most easily understood in terms of the Llancaiach Fawr case, it is also valid for the other two. A Broads' holiday and a meal in the Gudhjem Fish Smokery seek to interrupt the visitor's everyday experience in just the same way, and do so by replacing it with a similar yet different quality of life. Thus tourist service quality involves a satisfying interaction with people and artefacts from 'somewhere else', followed by a safe home-coming to the visitor's accustomed world.

Thus the cases described above demonstrate a subtle pressure upon tourist service employees to play the part of 'inhabitants of another world'. They have to represent the community in which visitors find them even if, as in Gudhjem, they may have only tenuous connections with it. The satisfaction and some of the motivation in such jobs are afforded by the creativity demanded by acting such a part. Only in the case of Black's Boatyard did this seem not to occur. The family were intent upon being themselves, and their employees seldom came into contact with customers. In this way the yard reduced the risk that their casual employees might upset or inconvenience customers, but in doing so they paid a high price. Llancaiach Fawr clearly demonstrated that suitably trained and motivated employees could build and improve the visitor experience to a high degree. Clearly the traditional sectors of this industry have much to learn from the newcomers.

Motivation

The popularity of university and college courses in tourism is widely ascribed to the industry's perceived glamour. Yet the three cases also demonstrate a dichotomy present in all such work. Fish smokeries and boat-yards alike demand a great deal of low-skilled and menial work. Alongside the 'glamorous' interpretational aspect of the heritage attractions industry is the routine of cleaning the toilets, waiting at table and basic administration. It would be easy to conclude that work in such operations has very little intrinsic motivation for the worker. However, this is almost certainly a misconception. Service staff at Gudhjem Smokery clearly enjoyed their contact with customers and the opportunities this presented for practising language and social skills. The fact that dirty work occasionally had to be done seemed to be a positive motivating factor at Llancaiach Fawr, reinforcing a team spirit that had already been built up through job rotation. Only at Black's Boatyard was there a lack of obvious team-work, and this seemed largely due to the family's desire to retain all roles involving managerial and interpersonal service work. Thus it would seem perfectly possible to motivate staff in small businesses of this type, but it is important to realize that the motivation is related more to the employment structure and to interpersonal relationships than to the content of the actual jobs themselves.

Team-working

Small tourism businesses are inevitably under pressure to perform as teams, in order to present a coherent service interface with the public. Of the three cases presented above, Llancaiach Fawr tackled the issue of team-work most effectively. This was done in part through the interpretation training, where it was explained that Llancaiach Fawr's style was to fix the time in 1645, wiping all later dates from collective memory. This presents staff with an immediate common challenge, since each individual's attempts to live in 1645 depends to some extent upon everyone else. In addition, the policy of rotating staff between 'departments' gave everyone a glimpse of others' problems and satisfactions, making it easier to achieve co-operation between them. These aspects reflected a coherent staffing policy. In contrast, Gudhjem Smokery made no special attempt to encourage team-work, but it arose anyway on an informal basis, owing to the proximity experienced while working. Probably the island connection of most of the workers also helped build a common feeling.

CONCLUSIONS

This chapter has presented three cases that seek to demonstrate how human resource management manifests itself in the small tourism business sector. This is a very diverse sector, containing both traditional and novel business concepts. As such, it has much historical 'luggage' to carry in terms of outdated or inappropriate management philosophies and practices. However, tourism is undoubtedly an economic growth area and is likely to remain dependent upon small entrepreneurs for some time. Its vibrancy means that it has the potential to refresh and sustain management thinking in the small service business sector in general, and not only within 'tourism' as defined in this chapter. The potential exists to energize small business development in all areas of tourism provision. However, to do this requires co-ordination, which at present is largely lacking. Existing small business associations mostly address the needs of one specific type of business, e.g. a region's tourist attractions, restaurants or hotels. There is clearly a need for associations, and perhaps also local government co-ordinating bodies, to take on a wider remit vis-à-vis destinations and resorts. In this way, among other areas of good practice, human resource management will be addressed.

REFERENCES

Berry, L. and Parasuraman, A. (1991), *Marketing Services: Competing Through Quality*. New York: Free Press.

Gyimothy, S. (forthcoming), Visitors' perceptions of holiday experiences and service providers: an exploratory study. *Journal of Travel and Tourism Marketing*, **8**(3).

Kozak, M. and Rimmington, M. (1998), Benchmarking: destination attractiveness and small hospitality business performance. *International Journal of Contemporary Hospitality Management*, **10**(5), 184–8.

Middleton, V. T. C. (1990), *New Visions for Independent Museums in the UK*. Chichester: Association of Independent Museums.

Waycott, R. (1995), Llancaiach Fawr living history museum. *Insights*, January, 25–33.

CHAPTER TEN

Seasonal Workers, Hospitality SMEs and the Employment Environment

Darren Lee-Ross

INTRODUCTION

The findings of organizational case study research are often perceived as being ungeneralizable even to other areas of the same industrial sector. Indeed, the case study aim of 'rich picture building' is often a tacit recognition by researchers that study conditions and variables may only be applicable to one specific case. However, a carefully designed research framework can increase the broader value of results in several ways. For example, an organization may be chosen which has similar characteristics to others. Moreover, fieldwork may be based upon several similar organizations, thereby increasing the generalizability of findings even further. If the extension of case study findings elsewhere is important, researchers must fathom a way to do it. Some may have insider knowledge of certain organizations, for example, because of earlier dealings as a former employee. More often, researchers rely on definitions (depending on the study area) to ensure similarity between organizations.

The present chapter deals with seasonal seaside hospitality small to medium-sized enterprises (SMEs). There are a number of definitions for each element of this composite area and students may be forgiven for thinking they are all designed to confuse. However, because of the human resource emphasis of this book, it seems reasonable to use employee numbers as a indication of whether an organization is an SME or not. The seasonal nature of seaside hotels also suggests that job tenure is an important consideration. In addition, other authors identify SMEs as family owned and operated. Indeed, this independence has a significant and identifiable bearing on enterprise strategy and operational procedures. Therefore for the purposes of this chapter, hospitality SMEs are defined as: *independent, family-*

owned seaside hotels operating between April and October of each year with 6–30 employees. Workers are mainly seasonal and hotels offer staff accommodation.[1] The chapter begins by outlining the historical development of domestic tourism in UK seaside resorts and its impact upon the emergence of hospitality SMEs. This theme is continued through the presentation of a case study for which research was undertaken over a four-year period. Permission was granted from hotel managers for findings to be published so long as anonymity could be assured. Therefore the Regency hotel is fictitious, and the substance of the study is an amalgam of features from six SMEs in the original case study.

DEVELOPMENT OF DOMESTIC UK TOURISM, SEASIDE RESORTS AND HOSPITALITY SMEs

According to Holloway (1992) the term tourism probably dates from the early nineteenth century. However, if parallels can be drawn from contemporary travel for the purposes of trading, business and religion, tourism happened much earlier in history. Holidays have their origin in holy days and therefore religion could have provided the framework within which leisure time was spent. Travelling requires several preconditions: speed, safety, convenience, and affordable comfortable transport. (Until the nineteenth century, transport enjoyed none of these things.) Early destination establishments were monasteries. The gradual development and improvement of lodgings in ale houses gave way to inns that were purpose built to meet the needs of stage-coach passengers. Places such as London, Exeter, and York became the first centres to attract visitors for pleasure purposes, and the wealth and social life of these cities were an attraction for the 'leisured' classes.

Transport systems and accommodation encouraged the growth of travel, but, equally important for certain people, was the *desire* to travel – for example as a pilgrim. Other factors contributed to the development of travel and tourism. For example, increased awareness and concern with health in the early seventeenth century led to the development of spa towns (Bath, Buxton, and Scarborough) due to the alleged benefits of the mineral waters. Over the ensuing 100 years, the character of these resorts changed, as pleasure, rather than health, became a popular reason for visiting them. The growth of stage-coach services to spas and other centres during the eighteenth century further enhanced their accessibility. Towards the beginning of the nineteenth century these areas expanded and attracted a new type of visitor: wealthy city merchants and 'professional gentlemen' rather than the earlier aristocracy and landed gentry.

By this time, sea water had been identified as containing the same minerals as spa water. This, coupled with the rise of the new pleasure-seeking visitor, led to the demise of spa towns and the rise in popularity of seaside resorts. Scarborough (the only spa town adjacent to the sea) was the first to exploit this trend, followed by Blackpool, Southend, Brighton, Great Yarmouth and other seaside towns. The cost of travel was at first prohibitive to most of the population but fell with the advent of steamboat services and the railway. These developments greatly helped popularize seaside resorts. For example, in 1815 a steamboat service began operating from London to Gravesend, and five years later, to Margate. One consequence of this development was the construction of piers at major seaside destinations. During the decade following the introduction of a rail link between Liverpool and Manchester in 1830, trunk lines were opened between major centres of population and industry. Later these were extended to include seaside resorts such as Brighton, making resorts accessible on a large scale for the first time.

Seaside towns emerged as holiday destinations in the early part of the nineteenth century. The authors of the 1851 population census identified them as one of four new types of town that owed their establishment and growth entirely to an 'industrial specialization'. Of the fifteen listed in the census, eleven were on the coast (Scarborough, Worthing, Weymouth, Brighton, Ryde, Cowes, Margate, Ramsgate, Ilfracombe, Torquay and Dover). Twenty years later their number had quadrupled. Most were still in the south of England, but in the north Scarborough was joined by Whitby, Fleetwood, Blackpool and Southport. By the end of the 1870s there were 45 urban seaside resorts, all with a common distinctive image (see Perkin, 1971) and all linked by rail to inland industrial centres. According to Patmore (1968) the distinctive image of resorts is due to their promenades, which function as attractions, and also defend the towns against erosion by the sea. In addition, resorts have rows of houses with sea views; concentrations of grand buildings on the seafront; railway stations located near the sea; and shopping streets. Other features originally established in the 1890s include grand hotels, winter and ornamental gardens, illuminations, tea-rooms, clock towers, bandstands and iron-work piers with pavilions and theatres. All of these attractions are usually sited adjacent to one other so that everything is accessible to people with no means of transport (Howell, 1974).

At the turn of the century, seaside resorts became popular amongst the working class, and all of them experienced a huge increase in demand.

Over the next few decades, large-scale capital investment was overtaken by small-scale development, characterized by the appearance of boarding houses, hotels, entertainments, and refreshment places. Holiday-makers who preferred greater exclusivity were displaced to smaller and less accessible resorts. Popular resorts expanded so significantly that for the first time the largest northern resorts challenged their southern counterparts. However, growth was maintained in many southern resorts between 1871 and 1911, particularly in Great Yarmouth. The economic recessions of the 1920s and 1930s stopped the growth in seaside towns, but by this time such resorts had enjoyed constant growth and prosperity for more than 100 years. Since the Second World War seaside resorts have lost their popularity as holiday destinations. Factors held responsible include private car ownership, the decline of the railways, and the advent of cheap, inclusive tour jet flights to warmer seaside resorts elsewhere.

CASE STUDY

Great Yarmouth is a resort town in the county of Norfolk in the Anglia region of the UK. It was chosen for the case study because it is a 'typical' seaside resort sharing similar characteristics with others established during the Victorian era. However, since the Second World War (and similar to other resorts) tourism has been in gradual decline because of increased competition from abroad. Nevertheless, income attributed to tourism as a whole for the Great Yarmouth area is around £18 million per annum. In terms of job creation, Great Yarmouth borough council reveals that approximately 8000 seasonal jobs are created in the area during a typical summer season, with 77 per cent of direct employment in tourism estimated as seasonal (GYBC, 1992, p. 34).

The stock of hotels in the town is around 200 and almost all of them are seasonal, independent and family owned. However, like other resorts, the SMEs of Great Yarmouth experience high levels of labour turnover during the summer months with employees frequently changing jobs for reasons that are often difficult for managers to fathom. This problem has obvious implications upon labour replacement costs and has associated impacts of reduced product quality. Tourists include pensioners, married couples, families and older teens. Hotel accommodation demand is mainly of the 'inclusive package' type (usually by liaison with coach tour operators) but also includes standard weekly and day room rates in response to direct contact with individual customers and to 'walk-ins'.

So far, this book has focused on a number of issues related to human resources and based on hospitality and tourism SMEs. Previous chapters explicitly or implicitly acknowledge that creating a 'reliable' workforce is essential if competitive advantage is to be achieved. They also recognize that motivating employees is fundamental in effecting high levels of service quality in the workplace. This is because of the essential role played by employees at the customer interface. Managers must therefore understand workers' attitudes so they can motivate them to provide high levels of service quality. While employee motivation cannot be underestimated in the present context, it remains a component of a larger, more comprehensive picture. Managers need to be aware of key environmental factors impacting upon their workers if they are to formulate effective, practical and continuing human resource policies. Clearly, some issues will have a greater bearing than others, but managers should adopt measures to ensure some labour market reliability and stability.

The present chapter takes the above for granted to avoid duplication and begins by focusing on the major motivational findings among employees at the Regency hotel. It continues by positioning attitudinal data within a broader perspective of some key 'external' issues already appearing in earlier chapters of this book. Finally, the concluding remarks include practical recommendations designed to assist managers in developing appropriate and practical human resource policies.

Regency case: background, working conditions and employees

The Regency is a two star (Automobile Association/Royal Automobile Club), medium-priced seafront hotel with 57 bedrooms (40 of which are *en suite*). The original hotel building was constructed towards the end of the Georgian era and the remainder was erected around the turn of the twentieth century. The hotel is essentially seasonal, closing during the winter months from November to March each year (except for Christmas week and occasional weddings, parties, association meetings and so on). The off season allows the owners and their core of six year-round employees to redecorate and refurbish for the forthcoming summer. Between April and October, core employees have managerial or supervisory jobs in the hotel. However, their job titles are notional, and almost all management activity is undertaken by the owners.

The workforce increases significantly during the summer season in direct response to customer demand. Recruitment and selection are unplanned, and often candidates are not interviewed but simply requested to turn up ready for work at a certain time. Many job vacancies are advertised in the local job centre approximately two weeks before the onset of business; most jobs are temporary and part time. In a minority of cases, newly recruited seasonal staff are related to, or friends of, core and returnee workers.

Operations at the Regency are characterized by a despotic, autocratic management style, with owners working for much of their time as operatives. Jobs are relatively unskilled, highly pressurized and low paid. Frenetic, crisis-type behaviour is felt necessary by owners because of the enormous pressure they face to 'turn a profit in such a short space of time'. The hotel offers no formal training to any staff. The hotel experiences high levels of absenteeism and labour turnover. This is unsurprising because many motivational models assume that 'favourable' working conditions lead to motivated workers who are less likely to quit their jobs (DeMicco and Reid, 1988).[2] However, most workers indicate high levels of motivation at work, but the focus is upon social bonding and forming relationships with co-workers. Many hotel employees care little for their actual jobs but value the chance their occupation gives them to be with like-minded people from similar backgrounds. (This phenomenon is also noted by Mars and Nicod, 1984; Ball, 1988; Riley and Dodrill, 1992.) Workers tend to form themselves into informal groups on the basis of residential status (living on or off the hotel premises) and work preference (whether they deliberately choose year-round or just seasonal work). Thus their residential status and work choice are key in explaining motivation and attitudes to work. For the sake of clarity, workers at the Regency may be divided into four subgroups. These are seasonal live in (SI); year-round live in (YI); seasonal live out (SO) and year-round live out (YO). Each group has different motivational preferences, and this is summarized in Figure 10.1. The horizontal axis shows the group members' affinity for hotel work, while the vertical axis is a measure of the individual's desire for social bonding with the group. The SI sub-group has a strong co-worker affiliation and tends to regard work-based factors as relatively unimportant. SO workers have little interest in hotel work itself but enjoy the convenience aspect of the job and the extra income it generates. Although the YI sub-group has strong work and co-worker affiliations, there is little difference between these employees and the SI sub-group. YO workers regard their work as important and therefore occupy a strong position along the horizontal axis, whereas co-worker affiliation is of little or no importance to them.

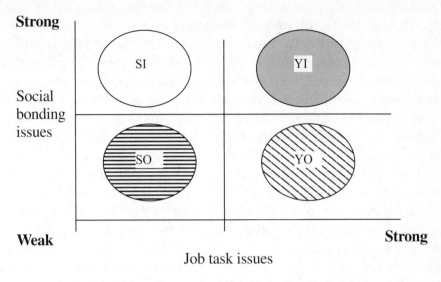

Figure 10.1 Matrix of sub-groups' preference for work-based and social bonding issues

---

INFLUENTIAL ENVIRONMENTAL FACTORS

Demographics

Tolfree (1990) and Beharrell (1992) estimate that by the end of the present century, the British labour force will have increased by approximately one million. This figure includes a projected rise of 2.3 million people aged 25–54, and a projected fall of 1.3 million in the labour force aged under 25. Consequently, the workforce will contain many more older people. In addition, the overall growth in the labour force will be in the service sector of the economy. Rather than being employed on a full-time basis, workers will probably have several part-time jobs. According to the Skills and Enterprise Network (1995) there is already a clear trend towards increases in part-time employment. The Employment Department (1996) observes that male unemployment within the East Midland and Anglia region is increasing at a higher rate than that of women; thus, the increase in part-time jobs has benefited more women than men. In addition, the above structural change has led to a need for training, particularly amongst workers who used to be employed in the declining manufacturing industries.

The Regency did not have problems with labour shortages, contrary to the findings of a recent Hotel and Catering Training Council (1994, p. 58) study. This shows catering and hospitality as having the highest percentage of hard-to-fill vacancies from a selection of industries. Beharrell (1992) suggests that to mitigate the impacts of the demographic time bomb upon organizations in future, more women, and more ethnic minorities should be employed. However, hotels have always employed a substantial number of these two groups in part-time and split-shift jobs. Typically this has meant that women form a substantial proportion of all hotel workers, because such jobs can be combined with family commitments. Although equal numbers of men and women were employed in the hotels of the present study, all of the part-time work was undertaken by women. An increasing number of 'new' women returnees might mean the rescheduling of full-time hotel jobs (so that they can be undertaken on a part-time basis), or the introduction of job sharing. This is likely to be more cost-effective for employers so long as the number of hours per week worked does not exceed the level at which the employer needs to make a contribution (see Contributions Agency, 1995). It may also be true that more women competing for fewer jobs will help both to improve the quality of the applicants and to keep wages at their current level.

Ethnic and foreign workers already form a sizeable proportion of all British hotel employees. Salt and Kitching (1990, p. 55) estimate that they form over half of all hotel employees in the UK. Salt and Kitching explain the preponderance of ethnic and foreign workers in the hotel industry on the basis of non-pecuniary benefits such as learning English and gaining experience or training. Interestingly, no ethnic minority workers were employed in the hotels of the present case study.

Training and employment

Training and employment are of paramount importance if competitive advantage is to be established and maintained. This is particularly true for the UK, a country generally perceived as offering jobs which are low skilled and low paid by comparison with the rest of Europe (Ashton, Green and Hoskins, 1989). Successive governments have launched several initiatives designed to minimize the training gap (in line with national training and education targets). These programmes attempt to reduce unemployment, and some are designed specifically for older returning workers.

New legislation designed to stimulate employment and job opportunities may also have an effect on the seasonal labour force. The most recent of these governmental programmes is the New Deal Initiative (1998) programme designed to expand employment opportunities by offering financial incentives and training opportunities. However, the motives and success of many government initiatives are open to interpretation. Beharrell (1992, p. 153) considers that they are primarily a way to optimize unemployment statistics and opines: 'they [government initiatives] are a convenient way to recycle the long term unemployed . . . and a significant distortion of the unemployment figures'. There is also an unfortunate assumption with such programmes that workers are willing to be trained or retrained. Typically, the 'structurally' unemployed worker is an older male with a history of employment in manufacturing industry. Such workers may find jobs in service industries unattractive, perceiving them as 'women's work'. Service jobs offer comparatively lower wages and this may also render them less attractive. The continuation of long-term unemployment looks extremely likely amongst this potential labour market.

These government initiatives may therefore force people into jobs either for which they are not properly trained or which they are unwilling to undertake conscientiously. This may lead to a demotivated hotel workforce and ultimately to higher levels of labour turnover. Programmes such as the New Deal Initiative (1998) may also exacerbate an existing problem of bogus unemployment benefit claims by some hotel workers. If people are forced into jobs that they would otherwise not choose, and particularly if the employment is low paid, there may be an increase in the above activity. This could effect greater labour turnover as workers increasingly fear being discovered by the authorities. To stem labour turnover, managers may decide to employ some of their workers unofficially, that is, employ them on a cash-in-hand basis to eliminate the need for official records.

The Employment Department (1996) places much of the responsibility for training upon employers and individual workers. This reliance on industry may be a problem because it involves employers changing their perceptions of the value of training. Industries dominated by small firms employing only a few employees, such as the hotel trade, are notoriously reticent to invest in training (see ETAC, 1983), perceiving it as unnecessary or too costly. In practice, such firms frequently offer no training at all; the Employment Department (1991) points out that only 18 per cent of small firms, mainly in the service sector, are training new or existing staff. In addition, since 1994, the overall picture of skill shortages appears to be increasing. than in 1994. This may be because of the government's desire to encourage the growth of small firms. The training gap may be further widened in industries where levels of labour turnover are high. The manager of the Regency said that even if he trained employees, the investment would be wasted because seasonal hotel workers usually quit their jobs after a short time. Most hotel job skills are transferable, and the results of training investment are often not enjoyed by the trainer, but rather by a different employer some weeks later.

In summary, government efforts have not resulted in increased training levels in hospitality SMEs for four main reasons:

1. naive assumptions may have been made by the government about the willingness of the workforce to be trained;
2. the reliance of government upon small businesses to provide wealth generation and training for their workers has been misplaced;
3. many small firms do not have the resources available for formal training, although some informal training may occur;
4. in the hotel industry many skills are not specific to one hotel, and because there is a high level of labour turnover, many employers will not invest in training.

Flexibility

The flexible firm, discussed in other chapters, has been advocated as the new style of commercial organization. It encompasses a situation where core workers, employed on a full-time basis, are multi-skilled, and where peripheral workers are employed on short-term contracts to cope with increases in demand. The flexible firm style of operation is standard practice at the Regency hotel. Core workers are employed on a year-round basis and peripheral seasonal workers are employed during the busy period to cope with increased demand. If flexibility continues it will undoubtedly benefit individual employers, but if workers continue to receive low wages, the local economy may become depressed.

Structural changes in the economy (Wells, 1989, p. 25) have created a need for training in service jobs, which are often part time and temporary. Workers need to be multi-skilled to take advantage of new job opportunities. The necessary training appears to be a priority of the present government, although the burden of its provision has mostly been placed on industry. Underlying the government's training and reskilling initiatives is the apparent need for workers (and SMEs) to be flexible, so that opportunities for employment and economic growth are maximized. The present government has tacitly approved this by leaving many changes made by the Conservative government untouched. For example, labour markets remain deregulated; certain legal elements of employee protection have not been re-established; wages councils have not been re-introduced; and growth of small businesses, rather than investment in large-scale industry, is encouraged. Whether this situation is morally desirable depends upon one's political beliefs. However, ensuring that workers have the ability to cope with a variety of work-related pressures and demands seems to make sense. Flexible, multi-skilled workers are also more valuable: in principle they can command relatively high wages, but this really depends on how skilled the jobs are in the first place. Jobs in hotels of the present case study were not highly skilled, and, as in other areas of the hotel industry, were comparatively poorly paid.

The Skills and Enterprise Network (1995) predict that firms will increasingly adopt a flexible structure using a core of long-term, full-time employees plus peripheral, short-term temporary workers (needed in response to fluctuations in the demand for their products). A survey by the Employment Department (1991, p. 12) shows that employers in the East Midlands and Anglia region are already beginning to adopt the idea of flexibility to cover peaks and limit long-term options. However, the idea of using core and peripheral workers is not new to the hotel industry. Many jobs are part time and of short, fixed duration. This is particularly the case in seasonal hotels, where core workers are employed on a year-round basis and seasonal staff are engaged during the busy summer period. Demographic changes are also impacting upon the workforce, and organizations will undoubtedly need to adapt to them in order to survive. Hotel managers will therefore need to be aware of the changes and how they might affect their organizations. Some of the likely effects of an ageing workforce upon hotel management are discussed below.

Older workers

Increased employment of older workers at the Regency may mean a reduced training requirement because employees already have some skills and experience. An ageing population will also probably increase the number of SO workers at the Regency, since older workers tend to be less mobile and therefore less willing to migrate to other areas for employment purposes. This potential increase in numbers is likely to have a deflationary impact upon wage costs, and skilled workers may be replaced with unskilled individuals. The Regency could deskill its operations, or conversely, may become more selective in recruitment because the competition for jobs will have increased. A falling demand for domestic holidays is likely to compound the issue.

According to Tolfree (1990), by 1998 there will be a fall of 1.2 million young people aged 16–24 in Britain to just under 20 per cent of the workforce. This trend will continue until 2000, albeit at a slower rate. There is also a projected rise of 2.3 million in the 25–54 age group. In theory, younger workers will be able to command a higher wage than currently by virtue of their reduced numbers. The Regency may therefore either have higher wage costs, or be forced to look elsewhere for its labour supply. Some employers may decide to replace expensive workers with new equipment, or the government may need to induce employers to recruit from other areas. However, the effect of fewer available younger workers (16–24) on the Regency is debatable because it employs comparatively fewer than other UK hotels (HCTC, 1994, p. 46). In addition, there is regular inward migration of workers to the Great Yarmouth travel to work area (TTWA). The Great Yarmouth Borough Council (1992, p. 30) predict that from 1990 to 2001 there will be an increase in the inward migration of 20- to 59-year-olds of approximately 10 per cent, while migrants aged 20 or below will fall by 5 per cent. In other words, the Regency does not rely on young employees, and will therefore be only marginally affected by this demographic change.

UK retailers such as Tesco, B&Q, Dixons and J. Sainsbury have employment policies that target older workers (Finn, 1990). Despite the HCTC's (1994) prediction that the training gap will increase owing to ageing of the population, older workers require less training by virtue of having more life experience and different priorities. They are more knowledgeable and tend to be better at the customer interface. Goddard (1987) considers older workers to be more reliable, have better life skills, and in general be better workers than their younger counterparts. On the other hand, because of the abundance of older workers, their wages may rise more slowly. This could have a negative impact upon their work attitudes and motivation because they may feel undervalued in comparison with the young. A concentration of older workers in an organization might also cause promotion blockages, thereby demotivating younger employees and increasing their level of labour turnover.

Managers of hospitality SMEs may be able to derive benefit from an older workforce in a number of ways. Labour turnover may be reduced because older workers are more likely to have families to support and hence are less willing to move out of the area (for example, to remove children from school). Older seasonal workers may also be more likely to return to the same hotel, especially if other employment is unavailable in the area. This may result in a more stable and experienced workforce. In addition, because these workers are returnees, they may have opportunity for increased informal contact with managers (in the workplace), and this may have a beneficial impact upon work motivation.

Workers at the Regency are older on average than in other sectors of the industry, and it may be argued that some of the benefits of employing older workers are already being enjoyed. This was certainly true for sub-groups having the highest average ages (YO and SO workers) whose members were mostly married with family responsibilities. Although these sub-groups valued their work for different reasons, both tended to remain at the same hotel and almost all of the SO sub-group were returnees. Conversely, if there are fewer younger workers available for hotel work, fewer older workers (especially in the 25–35 age group) will be replaced by them. Any difficulties the Regency may be experiencing with present workers (in the SI and YI sub-groups) are therefore unlikely to change. Although both SI and YI workers at the hotel seem satisfied with their jobs, they do not view the work itself as important, but see it as a means to an extensive social life with their co-workers. These motivational issues may be more difficult for a hotel manager to deal with because they are not based on work, and are therefore less easily controlled.

Staff accommodation and migration

The manager of the Regency addressed some of the 'problems' caused by live in workers (SI and YI) by minimizing the availability of staff accommodation. However, this tended to reduce some of the advantages of staff living in the hotel (for example, availability during times of 'crisis'). The manager added that it is sometimes difficult to replace all former live in workers (who view the accommodation facility as an incentive) with those living outside hotel premises. The manager thought that this type of staff shortage could be tackled by deskilling operations in order to broaden the potential labour market, but he worried about the detrimental effect this may have on the quality of the Regency product. The manager also considered concentrating exclusively on core activities, such as accommodation provision, and offering some catering operations to contractors. However, he thought that contractors would be unwilling to invest in an organization operating for only around six months of each year.

The Regency also faces a phenomenon of inward migration of workers from former industrialized conurbations. Currently, the trend is for such workers to remain unemployed in the area during the winter months. The presence of migrant workers has tended to increase the supply of DSS (Department of Social Security) housing in the Great Yarmouth TTWA. If migration continues, it is likely that the reduction of staff accommodation will help to fuel the demand for even more alternative DSS accommodation. This development is important because it means that former live in workers are now more likely to live away from the hotel premises. On the other hand, the manager thought that a saturation point would be reached. Increased competition from SO workers and the phenomenon of more local women returnees in the labour market would help slow the rate of inward migration. Thus SI and YI workers may eventually be replaced by their SO counterparts. Additionally, the manager said this would probably happen because live in workers 'were their own worst enemies'. For example, many were found to be apathetic and seemed unhappy with remuneration unless paid on a cash-in-hand basis.

The Regency's future workforce may also be linked to a wider movement of workers within the European Union. Some hotel jobs are low skilled and therefore the potential labour market is large. Hotel work is also low paid and less attractive to indigenous workers, but workers from European countries with a lower standard of living and high unemployment (for example, parts of Italy and Greece) may find the conditions acceptable. The manager considered that the Regency may attract a substantial proportion of workers from poorer European countries and introduce wider cultural motivational issues with which managers will have to become familiar.

The restructuring of the UK economy and the increasing importance of service industries as employers have changed the nature of jobs and the profiles of workers. Demographic change has also influenced the nature of the workforce in that employers may have to employ more older workers, women and ethnic minorities. Throughout the UK as a whole, the hotel industry already employs a substantial proportion of all three groups, although the Regency in particular had no ethnic or foreign workers. Increased mobility among European workers is likely to change this situation, and the manager thought that his supply of SI workers may increase as a result. He was also aware that this possible outcome may have a deflationary influence on wage costs, particularly if European workers originate from countries with a lower per capita income than the UK.

SUMMARY AND CONCLUSIONS

This chapter study has presented an apparent differentiation of hotel workers into four sub-groups organized by work aspiration and residential status. Whilst there may be some overlap between sub-groups in terms of their traits and characteristics, managers can at least be confident about some identifiable factors that motivate workers in each sub-group.

Owner/managers of seasonal hospitality SMEs experience many problems with their workers including unreliability, high labour turnover, theft, burglary and violent behaviour. In terms of human resources some may choose to do nothing at all, preferring instead to be buffeted by a labour market that supplies workers who are difficult to manage. Obviously, the options open to owner/managers of independent hotels must be practicable and cost effective. Strategies appropriate for year-round organizations often do not apply in businesses that generate only part-yearly profits, and that cannot offer job security or career opportunities for the majority of workers. To be of value, motivational initiatives must be capable of enhancing the organization in some way. They ought eventually to improve service quality, productivity and working relationships, and simultaneously reduce pilferage, absenteeism and labour turnover. However, the seasonal hospitality SME sector has the inherent difficulty of making enough profit during the season to ensure survival during the months of no revenue production. Pressure to generate this income is enormous and impacts upon every aspect of the organization. Therefore the industry will probably judge the value of motivational initiatives (whatever the criteria) over each single summer period, rather than in the long term. In addition, motivational initiatives will effectively be new every summer season for newly recruited workers. Seasonal hotels will therefore be unable to enjoy the economies of scale that occur in a year-round work situation. If motivational programmes are not perceived to be cost effective, subtle motivating factors, such as gradually increasing levels of responsibility, may be replaced by more direct measures, such as cash bonuses. Seasonal workers are likely to have a preference for this approach in any case. In extreme cases, managers may decide to do nothing at all about motivation, especially if there is a readily available supply of workers in the region willing to undertake deskilled hotel jobs.

Sometimes former YI workers become YO workers by virtue of their skills and capabilities. Whether workers' former aspirations remain with them once they make this transition is difficult to assess; this may be worthy of further study. Whichever motivational programme is implemented, it is

clear that difficulties will continue to occur if more than one set of preferences exist. Managers who at least recognize these basic worker differences
will be in a stronger position to motivate than managers who do not. In
addition to recognizing basic worker sub-group differences, managers
should also consider issues that are likely to affect the supply and structure
of the hotel labour market. An ageing population may lessen inward
migration to the resort area because of the extra family responsibilities
usually commensurate with older individuals. Therefore, SI and YI workers
may eventually be replaced by local SO workers. In addition, local women
returning to the labour market may also increase the potential supply of SO
workers. Employers may have to reschedule full-time jobs so that they
become 'convenient' to fit alongside family commitments.

Recommendations

In order for managers to motivate all workers in seasonal seaside hospitality
SMEs, they must first realize that they are dealing with a complex and
conflicting set of preferences held by a heterogeneous workforce. Each
worker has motivational preferences different from the other, and each
identified sub-group has a specific set of motivational preferences. It is clear
that one worker type resides in the TTWA and the other does not, though
increasingly members of the latter group are remaining in the region during
the off season. However, overall, both groups have different motivational
preferences. Within each of these two groups there are further attitudinal
differences, but in general YO workers are motivated by intrinsic elements
of their work, while the remainder are not. The SO, SI and YI groups are, in
fact, motivated by the work situation itself and the opportunity seasonal
work allows for indulging in close social bonding and other activities not
related to the job. Understanding these work attitudes is essential if managers are to motivate their employees.

There are two immediate courses of action which managers can take.
Year-round live out workers are motivated by intrinsic aspects of hotel
work, and these could be developed by increasing, where practicable,
aspects such as skill variety, autonomy and feedback. It may also be
worthwhile to develop jobs in this way for residential workers, because
some may eventually aspire to year-round career-oriented employment.
(This is, however, unlikely to motivate them because they have a preference
for factors based on the employment *situation*, such as the opportunity for
close social bonding and hedonism.) The other option that managers should
consider is whether to provide an employment framework that allows

workers greater accessibility to these preferred factors that are not based round work.

Before making recommendations it must be understood that any motivational strategies must be appreciated in terms of the depressed current position of tourism within the Great Yarmouth TTWA. Unsurprisingly, a recent report (GYBC, 1992) focuses on attracting visitors to the Great Yarmouth area rather than motivating its tourism-based workforce. By implication, the report suggests that if seasonality can be reduced and visitors with a higher spending power attracted, then some kind of systematic training can take place that will sufficiently motivate workers. The assumptions of the GYBC report are that hotel workers all aspire to year-round employment; that they have predictable attitudes to work; and that they can all be motivated by the same set of variables. (These assumptions are similar to the principles espoused by content theories of motivation.) This is clearly not the case among seasonal hotel workers. Training and motivational programmes based on simple assumptions are likely to fail. However, if seasonality can be minimized within the TTWA by investment from either the public or private sectors (or both), the need for seasonal workers will be correspondingly less. This may lead to a reduction of inward migrants to the area, and this will, in turn, reduce the requirement for DSS housing. It is also likely that there will be more year-round career opportunities in the hotel industry and this will attract more serious career-oriented workers. In the light of these results the present author makes the following recommendations, which can be broadly divided into the following three categories:

Strategic issues: central government

- initiatives could be set up that recognize the migratory patterns and transient nature of seasonal workers by allowing special 'benefit' dispensations. Alternatively, benefit sanctions could be imposed to discourage migration, thus eliminating the need for hoteliers to provide live in facilities and reducing the need for DSS accommodation in the town;
- linked to the former option, a register of seasonal workers could be created so that these workers could be targeted for seasonal job opportunities only. In addition, seasonal salaries could be augmented by a governmental financial adjustment, thus reducing the economic burden on the employers, reducing the significance of the black economy in the region and, one hopes, minimizing the desire for petty crime;
- a new hotel development scheme could be introduced in domestic seaside

resorts to encourage large hotel companies to invest in the area, thereby differentiating the product and attracting visitors with higher spending power on a year-round basis;

- the supply of seasonal labour could be changed by the extensive use of college students studying hospitality-based courses. Negotiation between industrialists and colleges could result in seasonal hotel employment becoming an integral part of students' educational programmes.

Strategic and co-ordinative issues: local government and hoteliers

- a committee of industrialists and representatives of the local tourism department should be formed to discuss the possibility of introducing standardized practical and affordable training and incentives schemes and to consider whether workers could be rotated around hotels. This committee could also draft plans of forthcoming human resources requirements;
- hoteliers should encourage representatives of the local tourism department to speak with their workers about any local training initiatives likely to benefit workers' career development in the industry;
- public and private services and amenities should be offered to seasonal workers free of charge or at a subsidized rate.

Technical managerial issues

- independent seasonal hoteliers could arrange to provide larger, year-round establishments with cohorts of trained workers at the end of the season. This may reduce training costs for year-round organizations and also provide seasonal workers with an opportunity for career development. In addition, this would provide seasonal hotel workers with a convenient step-off point, allowing them to choose between seasonal employment or a job that is more career oriented;
- several hotels could agree to share workers, thereby allowing workers social and work contact with a larger group and possibly allowing the development of new attitudes and skills;
- hoteliers could reduce the need for seasonal workers by creating more year-round core jobs and multi-skilling their workers;
- workers could be encouraged to 'take ownership' of the holiday experience through managers explaining to them that the non-pecuniary benefits they enjoy are also common to the holiday-maker;

- jobs requiring split-shifts such as food production could be rescheduled to eliminate this aspect, or could be shared by two workers on a part-time basis;
- some hotels could reduce their seasonal worker requirement by discouraging the food and beverage element of their organization through the use of appropriate pricing strategies (similar to hotels elsewhere that charge separately for accommodation and meals) or through the provision of accommodation only;
- workers could be offered more empowerment where practicable. For example, room attendants could be made responsible for ensuring each other's bedrooms were cleaned to an appropriate standard;
- hoteliers could encourage returnees by paying them a small regular salary during the winter months and also offer a 'subbing' facility similar to that enjoyed by workers during the summer;
- some workers could be given the opportunity to work in more than one department using similar skills. For example, waiting and bar workers could exchange jobs periodically. In addition, these workers could also be offered overtime in these departments;
- inter-hotel social and sporting events could be organized with the eventual responsibility being devolved to hotel workers. This may encourage a sense of team spirit and leadership and, most importantly, these would be developed away from the workplace. Thus workers (especially the SI and YI sub-groups) would be less likely to feel that they were 'selling-out', but rather, that they were taking responsibility for actions not based round work.

Notes

1 The author recognizes that many hospitality and tourism SMEs operate with far fewer employees than this.
2 Some researchers disagree and consider that the above relationship may be more complex than earlier models suggest (Deery and Iverson, 1995).

REFERENCES

Ashton, D., Green, J. and Hoskins, M. (1989), The training systems of British capitalism: change and prospects. In F. Green (ed.), *The Restructuring of the UK Economy*. Hemel Hempstead: Harvester Wheatsheaf.

Ball, R. M. (1988), *Seasonality in the UK Labour Market*. Vermont: Avebury.

Beharrell, A. (1992), *Unemployment and Job Creation*. London: Macmillan.

Contributions Agency (1995), *National Insurance*, Table 1, Not contracted-out contributions, 6 April 95 to 5 April 96, Social Security.

Deery, M. and Iverson, R. (1995), Enhancing productivity: intervention strategies for employee turnover. *Proceedings of the International Association of Hospitality Management Schools*, Sprowston Manor Hotel, April, vol. 1, pp. 1–15.

DeMicco, F. and Ried, R. (1988), Older workers: a hiring resource responsibility for the hospitality industry. *Cornell Hotel and Restaurant Administration Quarterly* [vol. unknown, no. unknown], pp. 56–60.

Employment Department (1991), *Labour Market and Skill Trends: Planning for a Changing Labour Market*. Nottingham.

Education and Training Advisory Council (ETAC) (1983), *Hotel and Catering Skills – Now and in the Future*, HCITB: Wembley.

Employment Department (1996), Pathways into employment. *Labour Market Review*, Winter, 1–19.

Finn, W. (1990), Grey matters. *Personnel Today*, April, 37–8.

Goddard, R. W. (1987), How to harness America's gray power. *Personnel Journal*, May, 33–40.

Great Yarmouth Borough Council (GYBC) (1992), A submission for regional aid for the Great Yarmouth travel-to-work-area, Great Yarmouth Borough Council.

Holloway, C. (1992), *The Business of Tourism*, 3rd edn. London: Pitman.

Hotel and Catering Training Council (HCTC) (1994), *Catering and Hospitality Industry – Key Facts and Figures*. Research Report, Hotel and Catering Training Council, London.

Howell, S. (1974), *The Seaside*. London: Studio Vista.

Mars, G. and Nicod, M. (1984), *The World of Waiters*. London: Allen and Unwin.

New Deal Initiative (1998), www.open.gov.uk.

Patmore, J. A. (1968), The spa towns of Great Britain. In R. P. Bekinsale and

J. M. Houston (eds), *Urbanisation and its Problems: Essays in Honour of E. W. Gilbert*. Oxford: Blackwell.

Perkin, H. (1971), *The Age of the Railway*. Newton Abbot.

Perrewe, P. C. and Anthony, W. P. (1990), Stress in a steel mill plant: the impact of job demands, personal control and employee age on somatic complaints. *Journal of Social Behaviour and Personality*, 5(3), 77–9.

Riley, M. and Dodrill, K. (1992), Hotel workers' orientations to work. *International Journal of Contemporary Hospitality Management*, 4(1), 23–5.

Salt, J. and Kitching, R. (1990), Foreign workers and the UK labour market. *Employment Gazette* [vol. unknown, no. unknown], p. 540.

Skills and Enterprise Network (1995), *Skills for Success: A Challenge for Training and Education*. Employment Department, pp. 1–7.

Tolfree, P. (1990), *Employees in the 1990s*. London: Croner.

Wells, J. (1989), Uneven development and de-industrialisation in the UK since 1979. In F. Green (ed.), *The Restructuring of the UK Economy*. Hemel Hempstead: Harvester Wheatsheaf.

Appendix

Sample product comparison checklist for HRIS

On the following pages are listed technical, functional and data requirements that represent the needs most commonly expressed by US business organizations. This checklist is by no means exhaustive, nor will it consider the 'special' requirements of individual organizations brought about by their industry, size, management style and/or employee policies and programs. No software system will meet an organization's needs without customization by the vendor, the user, or both.

This checklist is a place to start when comparing and contrasting various software solutions for human resources. Marketing information acquired on competing software solutions can easily be recorded and evaluated using this checklist, together with any customized additions, deletions, or modifications specific to the user organization.

TECHNICAL FEATURES	DESCRIPTION/COMMENTS
A Hardware requirements	
B Operating system	
C Local area network	
D Wide area network	
E Program language	
F Database manager	
G Client server	

HRIS FUNCTIONS	SAMPLE OPTIONS	SAMPLE OPTIONS
A Interfaces	❑ Payroll ❑ Time and attendance ❑ Benefits administration ❑ COBRA ❑ 401(k)/retirement	
B Integrated features	❑ Payroll interface ❑ Report writer ❑ SQL query ❑ Charts and graphs ❑ Import	❑ Export ❑ Organization charts ❑ Corporate roll-up ❑ Employee self-service
C Customization	❑ Data files (tables) ❑ Field, name, size, label ❑ Screen labels, colours, fonts ❑ Screens ❑ Screen layout	❑ Look up/calculation tables ❑ Menus ❑ Date/numeric range ❑ Edit logic
D Security levels	❑ Password ❑ Function access ❑ Module access ❑ Screen access	❑ Record access ❑ Field access ❑ Report access ❑ Data encryption
E Reporting	❑ Standard reports ❑ *Ad hoc* reports (unlimited?) ❑ Printers supported ❑ Presentation styles	❑ Report to screen ❑ Report to file ❑ Point-in-time reporting
F Utility functions	❑ Pending/future transactions ❑ Global add, update, delete ❑ Global recalculations ❑ Archiving	❑ Multiple currencies/ conversion ❑ Support for multiple languages ❑ Year 2000 ready

DATA MODULES	SAMPLE OPTIONS	SAMPLE OPTIONS
A Employee tracking	❑ Personal/demographics ❑ EEO, ADA, I-9, Visas ❑ Emergency contact ❑ Picture/signature ❑ Job data ❑ Organization data	❑ Payroll data ❑ Payroll forecasting ❑ Degrees, training, licences ❑ Safety/workers' compensation ❑ Labour cost calculations ❑ Employee survey management
B Benefits tracking	❑ Numbers of plans managed ❑ Comprehensive benefits ❑ Cafeteria benefit plans ❑ Dependants/beneficiaries ❑ Claims management	❑ Flexible spending accounts ❑ Employee benefits statements ❑ Awards and incentives ❑ 401(k) administration ❑ Stock programmes
C COBRA tracking	❑ COBRA tracking ❑ COBRA compliance ❑ COBRA invoicing ❑ Premium reporting	❑ COBRA eligibility dates ❑ Transfer to COBRA ❑ Generate COBRA letters ❑ COBRA dependants/ beneficiaries
D Time-off benefits	❑ Benefits accrual (vacation, sick) ❑ Track paid/unpaid time off ❑ Calculate plan balance	❑ Family/maternity leave programme ❑ Track by employee, plan, department
E Succession planning	❑ Position expense and headcount ❑ Track by employee, job, department	❑ Performance management system ❑ Identify back-up candidates
F Training administration	❑ Maintain curricula library ❑ Courses scheduler ❑ Site locator ❑ Equipment verification	❑ Assign instructors ❑ Enroll training candidates ❑ Update employee qualifications ❑ Notices, certificates, reports
G Employee self-service	❑ Employee handbook ❑ Update personal records ❑ View personal benefits files	❑ Relocation services ❑ Outplacement services
H Application tracking	❑ Job requisitions ❑ Job summary/posting ❑ Applicant personal data ❑ Test profiles/resume banks ❑ Reference checks	❑ EEO, ADA, I-9 ❑ Send letters, print labels ❑ Interview/contact ❑ Tracking ❑ Transfer to new employee module

Index